The Art of the Book in California: Five Contemporary Presses

Iris & B. Gerald Cantor Center
for Visual Arts at Stanford University

CURATED BY *Peter Rutledge Koch,*
Roberto G. Trujillo, and Alison Roth
ESSAYS BY *Robert Bringhurst and Peter Koch*

STANFORD UNIVERSITY LIBRARIES 2011

Published on the occasion of the exhibition:
The Art of the Book in California : Five Contemporary Presses
at the Iris & B. Gerald Cantor Center for Visual Arts at Stanford University

Studio photography by Douglas Sandberg.
Photographs of the printers courtesy of the presses.
Cover photograph : *Ur-text* by Jonathan Gerken.

Contents

5   FOREWORD   *Roberto G. Trujillo*

7   WHAT THE INK SINGS TO THE PAPER   *Robert Bringhurst*

27   THE ART OF THE BOOK IN CALIFORNIA: FIVE CONTEMPORARY PRESSES   *Peter Rutledge Koch*

THE PRESSES:
33   *Foolscap Press*
37   *Moving Parts Press*
42   *Ninja Press*
47   *Peter Koch Printer*
53   *Turkey Press*

61   PHOTOGRAPHS

109   A CHRONOLOGY OF FINE PRINTING IN CALIFORNIA   *Robert Bringhurst*

117   FURTHER READING

Foreword

It is a pleasure to contribute a foreword for the catalogue of *The Art of the Book in California: Five Contemporary Presses,* in which master printer and guest curator, Peter Koch, and the poet, art historian, and scholar of the history of typography, Robert Bringhurst, capture the significance and place in the history of printing these five printers and their books richly deserve. The Stanford University Libraries have collected the work of these presses since their inception, and in the past two years have been able to acquire nearly complete holdings from all of them. Collecting fine press editions and contemporary artists' books on an international scale has been, and continues to be, important for Stanford's libraries.

That an exhibition featuring the book as an object of art is being held at the Iris & B. Gerald Cantor Center for Visual Arts at Stanford is in no small part due to the creative vision of John and Jill Freidenrich Director Thomas K. Seligman. Tom was interested in collaborative programming between the Libraries and the Cantor Arts Center, and he wanted to find some way to showcase collections from the University Libraries in a museum setting. The exhibition partnership with the Department of Special Collections became a wonderful opportunity to share with the Stanford community a rich and diverse resource that has heretofore not been displayed as works of art.

Michael A. Keller, the Ida M. Green University Librarian and Director of Academic Resources at Stanford, has been no less enthusiastic about this exhibition, and more generally, about having these books available in the libraries to support research and teaching programs. The results of this genre of creative work have evolved over the last 25 years to become regarded today as art objects as well as books in their finest form. That we consider the book as a work of art is due in large part to the interpretation of text and illustration by the designer/printer. When successful, the maker informs the book's design, typography, illustration, material construction, and binding, rendering it luminous in the refined sense that Walter Benjamin described as the "aura" that an original art object has that a reproduction can never attain. The essays by Bringhurst and Koch place the books in the current exhibition within their art historical as well as their California printing historical contexts, thus speaking to the dual importance of these works in Stanford's collections.

Peter Koch, in his capacity as guest curator for the exhibition, was responsible for selecting the presses that are featured. Alison Roth, Assistant to the Director and Curatorial Liaison from the Cantor Arts Center, and I collaborated with Peter to make the final selection of books for the exhibition from the complete collections of the presses held by the Stanford Libraries.

Alison and her colleagues from the Cantor Arts Center, including: Holly E. Gore, Patience Young, Sara J. Kabot, Anna Koster, Margaret Whitehorn, and Katie Clifford were principally responsible for the overall management, design, publicity for, and installation of the exhibition. The curatorial responsibilities assumed by Alison Roth cannot be overestimated. The exhibition would not have been possible without Alison's interest, support, dedication, direction, and her critical eye as an artist. The design of the custom book cradles was done by Denise Fordham.

Any museum exhibition is possible only with extensive collaboration. In addition to the individuals noted immediately above, special acknowledgment is due Peter Koch, for whom the idea of creating such a project has been years in the making. Robert Bringhurst, in preparing his essay, spent several days at the Stanford

Libraries researching and consulting the works that would be on view. The context he provides deepens the importance of the project as he examines the history of printing in California and the evolution of the book as art object.

The Cantor Arts Center and the Stanford University Libraries have both relied on important financial support from endowed funds for this exhibit. Many of the books in the exhibit were acquired with The Morgan A. and Aline D. Gunst Memorial Library of the Book Arts Fund and the Robert L. Goldman Fund. Funding, in part, from the Cantor Arts Center came from the Clumeck Fund, the Drs. Ben and A. Jess Shenson Funds, and Cantor Arts Center Members .

ROBERTO G. TRUJILLO
Frances & Charles Field Curator
and Head, Department of Special Collections

What the Ink Sings to the Paper

ROBERT BRINGHURST

I

The printing of books came late to California – a thousand years after it first developed in China, four hundred years after Gutenberg revived it and transformed the mind of Europe, three hundred years after it was transplanted, with great success and style, to the Valley of Mexico, and two hundred years after the first press brought to North America began its tight-lipped work in Cambridge, Massachusetts. When printing did reach California, in 1834 – just before the territory passed from Spanish to Mexican, then to American jurisdiction – there was nothing especially fine or high-minded about it. It was employed almost entirely for bureaucratic purposes, in accordance with a principle enunciated several decades later in *The Hunting of the Snark*: what is said three times, or printed in multiple copies, must be and ought to be true. Printing had proven a subtle and powerful tool for preserving social fictions and maintaining civil order both in Madrid and in Mexico City. Surely it could do so in the provinces as well. But the times were inauspicious. Civil order collapsed; the press was left, very briefly, with no one to speak for and nothing to say.

Then came the Gold Rush. With it came a new and fervent appetite for spreading information (and, of course, misinformation) of many different kinds. In the 1860s and 1870s, California had dozens of letterpress printers churning out newspapers, books, magazines, certificates, handbills, and posters; it also had typefounders, stereotypers, engravers, color lithographers, editors, publishers, proofreaders, and a wonderfully multilingual assortment of booksellers. It had readers worth writing for, writers worth reading – including Mark Twain and Bret Harte for a time – and some very affluent and serious collectors.

The University of California's first campus, in Berkeley, opened in 1873. Eleven years later, the fledgling institution staged a massive show of celebrated books unmemorably titled the Loan Book Exhibition. There were 470 items on view, drawn from nine Bay Area public libraries, one club, and 67 private collections. They included, among other things, incunables from Germany, Italy, France, the Netherlands, and Switzerland, and sixteenth-century books from the presses of Aldus, Blado, the Estiennes, and Simon de Colines. There were also thirteen works connected with California. Eleven of these, however, were ungainly objects of purely historical interest (first known printing in California, first newspaper in California, first book printed in San Francisco, etc).[1]

In 1877, a book had appeared in San Francisco that was a kind of exhibition in itself. It was an album of color lithographs entitled *Grapes and Grape-Vines of California*. The publisher was an affable adventurer from Montreal, Édouard Bosqui (Edward to his English-speaking friends); the lithographer was a footloose Prussian who went by the name of William Harring. Bosqui was a man of many talents – painter, sculptor, engraver, bookbinder, printer. Printing seems to have interested him least among all these pursuits, but it was what provided most of his income. His specialty was engraved certificates, prospectuses, confidence-inspiring corporate by-laws and annual reports for the mining industry. He also did some vanity editions for well-heeled would-be poets. *Grapes and Grape-Vines*, while technically very impressive, is also a vanity book of a kind. Like many so-called artists' books and art books, it is a bundle of individual reproductions, "suitable for framing," and not a book at all as writers and readers use the term – not a complex, multi-dimensional structure in which time and space and thought get magnificently tangled in each other.

A few years earlier, Bosqui had printed a work of greater substance: a four-volume edition, in Spanish, of Padre Francisco Palóu's century-old *Noticias de la Nueva California* (1874). This was the first publication of the recently founded California Historical Society, and Bosqui illustrated it gracefully with albumen prints of photographs by Eadweard Muybridge, Charles Fessenden, William Rulofson, and others. There is nothing else like it in the long list of Bosqui's publications – evidently because the Historical Society foundered about the time the book appeared and did not really find its feet again until 1922. A copy of *Noticias* was the one book of Bosqui's included in the Loan Book Exhibition. It was also the only one of the 470 items described by the curators as a "fine specimen of California printing."[2]

Photography and chromolithography were exciting new media in the 1870s, but both were still slow and labor intensive. Type was still labor intensive too: finely sculpted little pieces of metal and wood, composed by human hands, one letter at a time. Yet handset type could be as fast for certain purposes as telephones and texting are today. In April 1871, when Ralph Waldo Emerson visited San Francisco, he was North America's best-known intellectual. Nevertheless, he had not expected fanfare in the wilds of California and had scheduled only a single public talk. He gave that talk on a Sunday night. At 11:00 the next morning, the printer Charles Murdock called at Emerson's hotel to ask if he would give a few more lectures before leaving town. When Emerson said yes, Murdock asked if he would be willing to give one that evening. After Emerson again said yes and a title was chosen, Murdock scribbled it down and went off. A handbill was typeset, printed, and distributed by newsboys on the streets that afternoon. The hall was full when Emerson spoke a few hours later.

The management and staff of almost any theater or gallery would scoff at such behavior nowadays. Instead of relishing its passion, they might call it unprofessional. People are too busy, they would say. Perhaps we are – or perhaps we're just too noisy, or too snarled in our noise. Yet serious writers and printers are still drawn to one another and have serious business to transact: the business of art, the business of thought, and the business of listening to the world, leaving something more than just a mined-out and desiccated planet for future generations. This not quite the same as the business of noise, nor is it the same as the business of territorial conquest and resource extraction. That serious but unaggressive business is why the press exists, and why the press is sometimes fine.

No one in nineteenth-century California was quite committed to the patient, subtle, perfectionist kind of work that printers, writers, and publishers call "fine." There were none of those devotees who see in a waking dream the particular letterforms, colors, and page shapes that a certain text demands, then nurture and nudge the type, the paper, the ink, and even the binding cloth and thread until they reify that vision and the letters start to sing. California in the nineteenth century lacked, on the whole, those sorts of "fine" or "impractical" writers, musicians, painters and sculptors as well. But it did have people hungry for what they were lacking. That is why, when Twain or Emerson passed through, a quick and sticky handbill could draw crowds.

Slower and less transitory printing began to coalesce in San Francisco in the final years of the nineteenth century, when Edward Taylor, a native San Franciscan, started his first printing firm and John Henry Nash, a self-important but talented typographer from Ontario, came to town. After eight years chafing as a journeyman, Nash went through several brief partnerships. The first was with another expatriate printer, Bruce Brough (who had left Toronto the year after Nash, and was still wanted there for unpaid debts); the next was with Paul Elder, one of San Francisco's several legendary booksellers; the last was with Edward Taylor and his younger brother Henry.

Henry Taylor was a fine typographer – in the end, perhaps, as fine as Nash, though he was no match for Nash in terms of pride and self-promotion. We may in fact have Nash's egomania to thank for the fact that Henry took time off from the new partnership to do some graduate work at Harvard. He enrolled in the School of Business, and did in fact receive an MBA, but he was also there for nobler reasons. Daniel Berkeley Updike was then on the faculty, teaching not just printing management but also typographic history. No one had taught that subject before, in a university environment, anywhere in the world. The course was disguised under the title "Technique in Printing," and Updike taught it in the business school, not in the department of art history, because business was his realm of officially recognized expertise. He owned and ran the Merrymount Press in Boston, and he had chosen to spend his earnings not on yachts and lavish vacations but on long, productive research trips to Europe.[3]

Soon after Henry returned to San Francisco, the partnership of Taylor, Nash, & Taylor was dissolved. Nash then opened his own composing room, where he specialized in vanity books for the wealthy, and the Taylor brothers continued, productively and peacefully, on their own, designing and printing what came through the door. Henry died at the age of 58, in 1937. His older and longer-lived brother retired in 1946, but the firm itself – a letterpress shop to the end – held its course until 1960.

II

In the decade after Nash and the Taylors had agreed to disagree, some other highly skilled typographers and printers set up shop in San Francisco. The most important, without question, were Edwin and Robert Grabhorn, who printed in their own immensely cheerful and creative and uncompromising way from 1920 until 1965. The Grabhorn brothers are rightly described as artist printers – not a term that can fairly be applied to Taylor & Taylor. The Grabhorns needed customers, just as the Taylor brothers did, but they did not permit their clients to tell them what to do. Nor did they flatter their patrons in order to flatter themselves, which is the essential problem with Nash. For the most part, they did what they thought was worth doing, in the way they chose to do it. Robert Grabhorn, the younger of the two, who did the bulk of the typography, rarely or never made sketches. "We let a thing grow," he said, "rather than design it."[4] His older brother, Ed, saw the process as "trial and error. Lots of times we halfway printed a book and then threw it all in the ashcan and started it

over because the idea was too silly to carry through."[5] Jane Bissell Grabhorn, Robert's wife, who was a capable printer herself and perhaps the most articulate member of that highly verbal family, put it this way:

There appears to be no organization, no planning, no system. Not only does the right hand not know what the left is doing, but the left hand has no idea what the hell it's doing either. In fact, when the Grabhorns are 'at work,' the general effect is of both hands being tied behind the back and two men walking around blindfolded. Then, suddenly, there's the book. Finished. I snarl, sneer, worry – but somewhere along the line someone must have been working. Because there's the book. Their teamwork is so successful that it is undetectable. Their combined talents are so perfectly synchronized that all appearance of effort as ordinary mortals know it is completely effaced.[6]

It is impossible, handling these books, not to realize that effort was involved, yet it is as she says: there is no *appearance* of effort. The Grabhorns were so good at what they did that people have tended to forget there were any other printers around. Memory, though, is worth some effort too. Among the contemporaries of Ed and Robert Grabhorn, we should remember not only Henry and Edward Taylor but also, for example, John Johnck and Lawton Kennedy: two printers who thought of themselves, correctly, as master artisans, not artists – but who drew out of their presses, day after day for decades, the same dependability of pitch, and the same richness and precision of intonation, that we expect a good professional violinist to produce from the violin. Without such people, art is nothing more than a pretentious monosyllable, and culture just a daydream.

Most fine printers, and the Grabhorns in particular, hold to a theory of truth like the one voiced silently by Keats's Grecian urn, not the one proclaimed aloud by Lewis Carroll's Bellman. They hold that truth is essentially beauty, not repetition. Notions of beauty do vary – so all fine printing is not the same – and repetition of a kind is certainly involved. The reproduction of beauty on the press in a limited edition is something dear to a printer's heart. It is an impulse with deep genetic roots. The alliance of multiplicity and beauty is a survival technique favored by plants and animals, not just by melodies, stories and ideas. But the repetition of one typographer's beautiful solution by another is something else again, more like subtraction than multiplication. Where no real growth takes place, beauty is smothered, not enhanced, by repetition.

The Grabhorns naturally set themselves apart from John Henry Nash and were often harshly critical of his work, though they sometimes bought his books, and they bought hundreds of pounds of his type when he closed his shop in 1938. In their turn, some of the Grabhorns' younger contemporaries complained that the Grabhorns' books were made to look at, not to read. One dyspeptic classicist of my acquaintance has even described their work as a "mire of post-Morris quasi-Venetian swarthiness."[7] That isn't quite how the Grabhorns saw it. What Ed Grabhorn said he was after was "strong, vigorous, simple printing – printing like mountains, rocks and trees, but not like pansies, lilacs and valentines; printing that came from the soil and was not refined by the classroom." And when he found what he was looking for, "the printer knew that the limited edition was not a racket as long as he had honesty and sincerity, and reverence for the best traditions of his craft."[8]

It is true that the Grabhorns were not the world's most diligent editors. Their books were nevertheless intended for serious readers far more than for idle spectators. They published real books by real authors and not, as a rule, trivial texts. And a Grabhorn page is a reader's page. It consists of good type well implanted in good paper, and very little else. Ornaments are few or nonexistent; illustrations, when they are present, are almost always subservient to the type instead of the other way round. And it has to be the right type, rightly spaced, in the right size. In this kind of printing, once the requisite typeface and measure (line length) are found, and then the requisite leading (space between the lines) and page depth (number of lines on the page) are found, the book is nearly done. Poets spend a lot of time looking for exactly the right syllables and silences, composers for just the right pitches and intervals, note values and rests. Silly as it may sound, typographers spend just as much time searching for just the right small shapes of black with the right small empty shapes between them.

Printers in San Francisco throughout the twentieth century were fortunate to have more type and better type than many printers elsewhere. Before that century began, the city also quietly revolutionized the way in which typographers and printers throughout the English-speaking world handled, stored, and measured the type they used.

Foundry type is laid in cases – partitioned wooden trays with compartments of varying size and shape. The earliest European cases were almost certainly arranged with all the letters in a single tray. By the seventeenth century, however, many compositors working in the Latin alphabet (especially those who worked in English) laid their cases in pairs and racked them one above the other. Caps (and usually small caps), as everybody knows, went into the upper case; small letters, punctuation, and spaces went into the lower case; numerals and ligatures went either up or down. In the nineteenth century, however, many compositors started experimenting again with single cases, especially for advertising work – then known to printers as jobbing. By far the most successful new single-case design was one manufactured in San Francisco by Simons & Co., starting in the early 1870s. Octavius Dearing, who had come to California from Maine around 1871, promoted this case aggressively and may have had a hand in its design. He liked to hear it called the Dearing case, but compositors then and now have preferred to call it the California job case. By the end of the nineteenth century, it was popular enough that compositors tended to use it for book faces too. Letterpress printers from Florida to Alaska and Los Angeles to New York are using it still.

Systems for type measurement also go back to the beginning of typographic time – but the system now in use throughout the English-speaking world is another product of nineteenth-century San Francisco. Nelson Hawks came to the city in 1874 to establish the Pacific Type Foundry. Three years later, he published his new measurement scheme, with twelve points to the pica and six picas to the inch. This simple plan was wrinkled slightly in 1886, when a meeting of foundry owners decided that six picas should be four thousandths short of a full inch, but with this modification, Hawks's system is still standard in North America and Britain wherever metal type is used. (For digital type, we have reverted to Hawks's original scheme – and that decision too, as a matter of fact, was propagated from California.)

Frederic Goudy, who for decades was the world's only full-time independent type designer, visited California often in the first half of the twentieth century. The Grabhorns used his types extensively. They even bought exclusive rights to one of his faces and christened it Franciscan, in honor of the city where they worked. Goudy designed two other text faces specifically for California patrons. One of them, designed for the University of California Press in 1938, is one of his greatest successes.

It was a good day, too, for San Francisco printers when Carroll Harris came to town. Harris had been a rising star in the management of Lanston Monotype, headquartered in Philadelphia. (Lanston, along with its sister firm in England, manufactured Monotype typesetting machines and the matrices they use. Monotype machines produce a close approximation to handset type, and they produce it in the same physical form as handset type: each letter cast on a separate block of typemetal. A skilled compositor can edit, correct, and refine type set on a such a machine just as if it were set by hand.) Harris – fondly known in later life as Colonel Harris – was a West Virginian of military bearing who had fallen in love with France, married a French woman, and amassed a fine collection of French books. After 1919, when he saw the West Coast for the first time, he was in love with California too. In 1923 he resigned from Lanston and settled in San Francisco. There he went to work for George Mackenzie, whose typesetting company used a rank of the Lanston machines. Three years after Harris joined it, Mackenzie's firm was reborn as Mackenzie & Harris. Over the next thirty years, under Harris's control, M&H became the Western States agent for a number of European typefoundries and developed the finest collection of matrices for text type to be found in North America.

The shapes of letters are concrete and formalized traces left by the dance of the speaking hand. As such, they are meaning incarnate, like musical notes, and yet they function as abstract symbols for spoken sounds. They are primary facts, yet, at the same time, they are symbols twice removed: representations of representations of meaning. To put it more simply, they mean what they are as well as whatever, in this or that language, they happen to say. And they can resonate with other shapes and textures, far outside the alphabet, that are also meaning incarnate. This happens most clearly when letterforms are placed near other objects, other shapes, that have some of the starkness and simplicity and purity we associate with letters.

Such shapes occur in nature, and in artifice, and in art. They commonly occur in rocks and trees, as Ed Grabhorn suggested, and in elemental manufactured objects such as bricks, boards, tiles, and simple tools. In art, this kind of purity and starkness is associated mostly with ascetic, uncolorful media. In the early days of printing, both in Asia and in Europe, typographers found such visual counterpoint not in gilded illumination but in the woodcut. In more recent times, typographers have often turned to the woodcut again – and of course to line drawings, now that these can be photomechanically reproduced. They have also turned to black and white photography. More importantly perhaps, some of the world's finest black and white photographers have repaid the compliment, asking typographers to create an accompaniment for their photographs.

Ansel Adams – a skilled pianist as well as a great photographer – knew very well how counterpoint, polyphony, and harmonic accompaniment work. He was also deeply interested in the nature of the book, and he understood from early in his life how a sequence of visual images – especially when pared down to black and white – could constitute a structure unfolding in time, like a sonata or toccata. Examined as physical objects, books appear to be devices that hold sequences together. Contemplated as essences, books turn out to be sequences that, by the force of meaning, *hold themselves together*. The physical book is what it is and does what it does because that is its essence, its nature. California, where Adams was born and did much of his work, is where most of his finest books were produced, both conceptually and physically.

A photographic book may or may not include much text. What it must include is a suite of images that resists dismemberment: images whose sequence is rhythmic enough, melodic enough, and tight enough to be more than the sum of its parts. Adams's first venture into this domain was a portfolio of eighteen photographs which he assembled at the urging of a patron, Alfred Bender, in 1927. The Grabhorns designed and printed the few pages of text, and Adams made the prints by hand in his darkroom. The prints were loose and easily removed from the portfolio, but their relation to each other was still declared: they formed a numbered sequence. The publisher, Jean Chambers Moore, contrived to muddy this a little by giving the portfolio an Edward-Lear-like name, *Parmelian Prints of the High Sierras.*[9]

Adams's next such venture, *Taos Pueblo* (1930) is more crisply titled and more obviously book-like. The prints (only twelve this time) were again made individually in the darkroom, not printed on a press, but they were made in a printerly fashion: exposed and developed directly on book paper which had been treated with a photographic emulsion. There is a substantial textual accompaniment, written by Mary Austin, printed letterpress on exactly the same paper (minus the emulsion). Text pages and photographic pages are bound in the same way, and flex and turn in the same way, and so they flow with a similar motion. We are encouraged to *read* the images, and to read them as a sequence, not just to look at them one by one. Adams himself served as the publisher this time, and the Grabhorns designed and produced the physical book.

Eight years later, the mechanical printing of photographs had advanced to Adams's satisfaction, and he produced an artist's book relying entirely on letterpress. This was *Sierra Nevada: The John Muir Trail*, designed and published in Berkeley by Wilder Bentley.

Wilder and his wife Ellen set and printed the text, though the fifty tipped-in images were printed in Chicago.[10]

III

The distance from Ozorków to Warsaw is about the same as from Monterey to San Francisco or Santa Barbara to L.A., but Saul Marks, who left Warsaw at age sixteen (when his name was still Yisroel Chaim Miodownik), and Lillian Simon, who left Ozorków at age four, had to find their separate ways through the maze of modernity before meeting one another years later in Detroit. Then they learned that, if the world had been more peaceful, they might instead have met (or not have met until it was too late) at a Bar Mitzvah or a market close to home. They also had to move, as newlyweds, to California in order to discover that their future lay in running a small fine press. The Plantin Press, which they founded in Los Angeles in 1931, turned out crisp, handsome work for more than fifty years.

Gregg Anderson, Grant Dahlstrom, and Bruce McCallister had begun to make fine books in the Los Angeles vicinity when Saul and Lillian Marks arrived. So the Plantin Press was not perhaps the first fine press in Southern California, but it proved the most consistent, productive and long-lasting. It also embodied, as no other press ever has, a crucial aspect of California culture. The Markses were immigrants in a land that was simultaneously barbarized and blessed. They knew that this was so, and they had not come hoping to get rich but hoping to take refuge. They knew full well that the printed word could not create or even preserve civil order, but they knew that, with sufficient love and care, it can generate some light. Many other dislocated people in twentieth-century Los Angeles felt the same: Thomas Mann, Bertolt Brecht, Arnold Schoenberg, Bruno Walter, Igor Stravinsky, Hanns Eisler, Franz Werfel, Alma Mahler, Alfred Döblin, and Erich Maria Remarque, to name a few. The Markses printed a great deal of Californiana; they also printed art books (real ones — such as

Andrew Ritchie's *Abstract Painting and Sculpture in America*, for the Museum of Modern Art, in 1951); they printed (for themselves) Saul Marks's homage to Christophe Plantin, and (for Lawrence Clark Powell) Yehudi Menuhin's to Béla Bartók; but they stand out among California presses for one thing above all: printing significant new work by Thomas Mann, Franz Werfel, Alfred Döblin, and other refugees who were, at the time, their immediate neighbors.[11]

In San Francisco, Lewis and Dorothy Allen, contemporaries of Saul and Lillian Marks, started printing together in 1939 and continued without interruption until 1992. The immensely industrialized war raging around them at the start of their career left them eerily untouched, and working entirely by hand became for them a kind of religion. Printing on the handpress thus became a vocation to be carried wherever they went. They were never refugees, but theirs was surely the most peripatetic fine press ever to function in California. In more than half a century of work, they printed north, south, east and west of San Francisco Bay; they also went to Florence to print Shelley's *Ode to the West Wind* and to the French Riviera to print Poe's *Murders in the Rue Morgue* and Robert Louis Stevenson's *La Porte de Malétroit.*

As the Markses arrived in Los Angeles, another fine-printer-to-be was just leaving. His name was Ward Ritchie. He was on his way to Paris, where he printed a poem by Robinson Jeffers under the tutelage of François-Louis Schmied, the impassioned, one-eyed master of a style of illustration and typography now known as Art Deco. We should take care not to trip on the label. Schmied and his colleagues never spoke of their work as "Art Deco." The term was not coined until the movement was already over. To those who created it, it was simply *le style moderne.* Jeffers, looking back in his late forties, claimed that in his twenties he had flatly decided "not to become a 'modern'." Ritchie, who entered his twenties twenty years later, admired Jeffers greatly, but Ritchie went to Paris precisely to learn to be *moderne.* He did not, however, go to Paris to learn to be Schmied. His work is sober in comparison with his teacher's – much less colorful and much less geometric.

Master and student were quite different in both temperament and talent, yet I believe Ritchie was right to think that Schmied had something to teach him. Schmied was born and trained in Geneva. His books are engineered as carefully as clocks, though many who see them notice only their jewelled faces. He had never been to North America, much less to California, but Schmied was just as interested in spectacle as Cecil B. DeMille. He had lost his eye at Cappy, on the Somme, fighting with the French Foreign Legion, and he knew as well as anyone in Hollywood how much military discipline is needed to make a spectacle happen as planned.

The Second World War not only brought a lot of intellect and talent to California; it also took a lot away. Gregg Anderson, for instance – possibly the most talented, and certainly the most broadly trained, fine printer in Southern California – was killed on the beach in Normandy in 1944. Anderson had taught himself the rudiments of typography and presswork as a boy. Then he got the kind of job that every aspiring printer should get but almost never does. Directly out of high school, he spent a year sorting and cataloguing fifteenth- through twentieth-century books at the newly constructed Huntington Library. At the same time, he was tutored through the mail by a celebrated perfectionist, Porter Garnett. (Garnett was a native San Franciscan teaching at Carnegie Tech in Pittsburgh, where he founded and ran the Laboratory Press. He is a central, if nearly invisible, figure in California printing, because of his religious devotion to the craft and the number of Californians he taught. Anderson, however, is the only one I know of who studied with Garnett by correspondence.)

After printing briefly on his own in Pasadena, Anderson moved to San Francisco and worked for two years with the Grabhorns. After that, he spent three years in Connecticut, running the letterpress shop at Meriden Gravure – then perhaps the finest place in North America to learn the art of printing images. After his return to California in 1935, he and Ward Ritchie formed a partnership that endured until Anderson died. One of the things that happened to Anderson as he matured was that he grew impatient with the *niceness* of much of the fine printing he met. It was biased toward the visual and away from the linguistic; it used the linguistic for visual ends; it was often laden with nostalgia for the printing of bygone days; the scholarship and proofreading were very often poor; and fine printers often preferred amusing trifles to meaty and serious texts. These complaints were not new in the 1930s, nor are they old and stale now. That is why printers like Anderson are so important: hunting for alternatives to trivia and shallowness is never a waste of time.

Like most people who truly love to learn, Anderson was also always teaching what he knew. During a stint at Pomona College, for example, he learned some things about fortuity and music from his iconoclastic roommate, a young composer named John Cage – and Cage later said that it was Anderson who proved to him the value of representing musical structures in custom-tailored graphic form.

IV

There are three California fine printers of particular importance who started serious work during or just after the Second World War. Each had help, sooner or later, from knowledgeable elders, but each still had to find his way in a society deeply unsettled and depleted by the war. These three are William Everson, Jack Stauffacher and Adrian Wilson. Some others might be grouped with them, including Andrew Hoyem, founder of the Arion Press, and James and Carolyn Robertson of the Yolla Bolly Press, though younger they did not begin to print until well into the time of another, more puzzling war, whose epicenter was Vietnam. Everson, Stauffacher, Wilson, and also Hoyem seem to me of notable importance in themselves; they also served as teachers and mentors to several printers in the present show. In varying degrees, all four of them have guided me as well.

Bill Everson was born in Sacramento in 1912 – only four years later than Gregg Anderson – yet in practice he belonged to a different generation. He pursued four distinct and demanding vocations: poet, printer, lover, and monk. His devotion to each calling was absolute, but it is costly, fitting four lives into one, and his development, jumping from one to another, was slow. He looked like a Taoist sage, ancient beyond counting, for the last two decades of his life, yet he was passionately boyish even at eighty, a year before he died. His mother was a typesetter; his father was a printer and a traveling musician of the marching band persuasion. Everson was setting type, feeding a press, and distinguishing musical keys as a small child. Yet both his parents, according to their son, embodied "all the innate American hostility to the artist." Not until his early thirties did he address himself to the practical techniques and basic moral principles that distinguish fine from ordinary printing.

Jack Stauffacher was born in 1920 in San Francisco. He is turning ninety and still working in that city as I write this. His father was a plumber, but of a wonderfully civilized kind: one who tended his grounds and garden with loving care, was delighted instead of intimidated by art, and encouraged his children to do what they loved. Jack was raised in San Mateo, where he fell in love with printing just as he entered his teens. Updike, he says, was his first teacher – meaning that, like many of us, he read, cover to cover, the two volumes of *Printing Types: Their History, Forms, and Use* – the book that grew out of the lectures Henry Taylor had attended in 1915–17. At the ripe age of sixteen, Stauffacher designed and built a pressroom of his own, just behind the family house and established his Greenwood Press. By then he was also paying visits to John Henry Nash, the Grabhorns, and the Taylors. Stauffacher's early books prove that, even in his early twenties, he had developed a mature sense of typographic space, fine control of inking and impression, literary taste, an historical sense of type and text, and a lively imagination – in other words, most of the moral and mental equipment a serious printer requires. This dream was interrupted in 1942, when he was conscripted. He then spent two unwilling years in Kentucky and Texas doing military cartography. In 1955 he left California again to spend three years in Italy immersed in Renaissance books. Then he taught in Pittsburgh, where he discovered and restored the forgotten legacy of Porter Garnett. In 1967 he returned to San Francisco and reopened the Greenwood Press – and he has functioned ever since as California's irrepressible typographic conscience.

Adrian Wilson was born in Michigan in 1923 and raised largely in Massachusetts. His parents were Dutch immigrants – Dutch remained the favored language of the house in which he was raised – and his father was not just a gardener but a professional horticulturalist. (There is some evidence here that gardens are good places to grow typographers.) Dutch Protestantism, which can thrive in gardens too, forms a recalcitrant part of American Puritan tradition, but Wilson's upbringing was not of that kind. His letters to his parents, written in his late teens and early twenties (and published after his death), are so articulate, so mature, so rich with open and sophisticated references to literature, chamber music, dance, theater, ethics, and sexual relations, that they qualify not only as un-Calvinist but as downright un-American.

Wilson knew nothing whatever of printing until he and Everson met in a work camp for conscientious objectors – Camp Angel, near Waldport, Oregon. Everson was assigned there in the summer of 1943, Wilson a year later. (It appears, in fact, that Wilson set off on his journey from Massachusetts to Waldport on 5 July 1944, which is the day Gregg Anderson was killed.) At Camp Angel, when they were not planting trees or doing other prescribed chores, Everson, Wilson and several friends printed broadsides, pamphlets, and books under the imprint of the Untide Press.

If Stauffacher had known how to formalize his own quite ardent anti-militarist impulse, he might have been there with them – to everyone's great benefit. As it was, the printing Wilson and Everson did at Camp Angel, while inventive, was not especially fine, because Everson himself, the printer's son, a decade older than Wilson, had not yet fully grasped that printing was an art. Wilson and Everson graduated from printing to fine printing only in the later 1940s, in Berkeley and San Francisco, with the war and the camp behind them. It was there that they first encountered a few printers – Stauffacher, Wilder Bentley, and the Grabhorns – of the kind they would become.

From 1947 to 1958, Everson printed in Berkeley and Oakland under three different imprints: the Equinox Press, Seraphim Press, and Albertus Magnus Press[12] – a progression that reflects his increasing engagement with the Dominicans, of which he was a member from 1951 to 1969. From 1971 to 1982, he printed at Santa Cruz under the Lime Kiln imprint. Most of what he printed was his own fine poetry, but the books that are routinely cited as his greatest achievements in printing are an incomplete edition of the Latin Psalms (1955) and Robinson Jeffers's *Granite and Cypress* (1975). After 1982, his Parkinson's disease prevented further work. He died at Kingfisher Flat near Santa Cruz in 1994.

Wilson and Stauffacher were partners very briefly in 1948 – a relation that ended amicably and quickly because both men needed to make some money and both could do it better alone. Wilson's way of doing this, for most of the rest of his life, was by designing books he usually didn't print. He could envision a work clearly, foresee the technical problems it would raise, and specify, in efficient, professional language, not only what he wanted but how it could be achieved. This is the antithesis of the method favored by the Grabhorns. Yet Wilson's exuberance, his impish delight in creating new problems and then finding their solutions, and his love of layered and open asymmetry rather than closed, symmetrical forms, make it clear that he was the Grabhorns' true successor. When he died in 1988, he had done more than anyone else in North America to blur the boundary between fine and industrial printing – and had done this chiefly by raising the bar and banishing stuffiness on both sides.

In one of those letters to his parents, written in December 1946, Wilson had stated his aims in the most unpretentious terms. They were "to know I am doing something which is beautiful both in what it is saying and in its typography, and to know that I am not just filling up the world with more crud."[13] Like Anderson, however, Wilson came to understand that in aiming consciously at beauty we often arrive at something else, of lesser value – something dangerous, in part because, in all but the most careful speech, it very often goes by beauty's name. One can emasculate a book – and possibly insulate people from literature as a whole – by making the book too *pretty* or making it too *nice*. On the 1st of May 1948, Wilson and Stauffacher visited Albert Sperisen, an eminent collector. Adrian wrote to his parents the next day.

Saturday afternoon Jack and I went out to the leading local bibliophile's house to look at his collection.... Of course it was completely dazzling to us and we left reeling. Every word we uttered, he had a book for it.... There is of course a danger in this: we lose sight of the purpose of books in making them beautiful. But if the words are good enough they can stand a tremendous amount of artful treatment, craftsmanship, and repetition. It is still my purpose to make people read less better, instead of more faster.[14]

Concealed in that abbreviated statement is the ultimate agenda for fine printing: reading less and reading it better. And in reading less, to make sure that what we read, most of the time, is the best there is. Not necessarily the prettiest but the most enlightening, most trenchant, most sustaining – which ought by rights to be the most beautifully written. In a perfect world (which we are always going to make as soon as the latest war is over) the best musicians would be playing the best music, the best writers would be writing the greatest literature, and the best printers would constantly be occupied setting and printing what all the finest writers have written. But in fact the world is a complex place, and in seeking perfection we are sometimes driven to devious means.

Andrew Hoyem was born in South Dakota in 1935, the son of a physicist. In 1946 he moved with his family to the naval weapons testing range near China Lake, California. A few years later he was studying literature and art at Pomona College. He then served three years as a junior naval officer – but much of his navy time was spent reading hardcore modern poetry at a landlocked air force base in Texas. In 1961 he moved to San Francisco, where the poets he'd been reading were largely to be found. He soon joined Dave Haselwood's Auerhahn Press, a fledgling printing and publishing operation that dealt in almost nothing but beat poetry. Haselwood knew little about printing, and Hoyem knew even less, but both of them – Hoyem especially – learned as they went.

In 1965, Hoyem bought Haselwood out and started working on his own, initially calling his operation the Auerhahn Society.[15] Though essentially self-taught, he was adept enough by then that the Book Club of California asked him to print a suite of keepsakes. He hung out a new sign saying "Andrew Hoyem, Printer." But the Grabhorn Press, his famous neighbor, also closed its doors that year, when Edwin Grabhorn decided to retire. His brother Robert, eleven years younger, was therefore looking for something to do. In 1966, Robert Grabhorn and Andrew Hoyem formed a partnership that endured until Robert's death in 1973. Hoyem then acquired the Grabhorn Press's considerable collection of type and equipment. With that endowment, he founded his new imprint, Arion Press. Sixteen busy years later, he also bought the Mackenzie & Harris typefoundry and Monotype shop, renaming it M&H Type. At this point, Hoyem owned one of the two or three finest and largest typecasting, typesetting, and letterpress operations to be found in North America. He also owned the monumental problem of keeping this facility housed and fed. Part of his tactic for doing so has been to specialize in luxurious editions of celebrated texts. He has published, for example, the Bible, *Moby Dick, Ulysses, The Great Gatsby, The Maltese Falcon,* and *The Waste Land.* In 1979 he also published a sumptuous bicentennial edition of the U.S. Constitution. Many of the books are illustrated by renowned visual artists. (Robert Motherwell, for instance, did *Ulysses*; R.B. Kitaj did *The Waste Land.*) Each year there have also been some arcane texts and little-known authors in the list, but clearly the famous names have been essential to paying the rent. By this means, Hoyem has become the one fine printer in North America flying at the economic altitude of a sizeable trade publisher. He has now, as he reminds me, been printing and publishing for fifty years. What the future holds for the Arion Press I do not know, but Hoyem has wisely and generously sheltered its irreplaceable hoard of material and machinery under a nonprofit entity called the Grabhorn Institute.

William Everson, Adrian Wilson, Jack Stauffacher, and Andrew Hoyem are, as it happens, the last four of the sixty-odd printers and typographers discussed at length in Joseph Blumenthal's grand historical survey *The Printed Book in America* (1977).[16] No one has written a book of that caliber on the subject since – but in 1975, in San Francisco, Sandra Kirshenbaum began to edit and publish a quarterly journal known as *Fine Print: A Review for the Arts of the Book*. The journal did not restrict itself to American fine presses, much less to presses in California, but it gave excellent coverage to these regions, and its reports began essentially where Blumenthal left off. *Fine Print* ceased publication in 1990 (coincidentally, the year in which Blumenthal died). Other journals have tried to fill its shoes,[17] but we have not yet had another Blumenthal, nor another Kirshenbaum either.

V

Books, as Sandy Kirshenbaum often observed, do not much like museums. They do not like to be locked down under glass, where they cannot feel their pages being turned and are thus prevented from doing their work. Some are less gregarious than others, but what all books seem to like when the time seems right is interacting with readers, writers and ideas: participating actively in the sensual life of the mind. I doubt that books remember being written, any more than humans remember conception or life in the womb. But if their typographers, pressmen and binders know what they're doing, I am willing to bet that books may also enjoy being printed: becoming embodied, or reembodied, so that their sensual life can unfold.

Nevertheless, it is arguably true that there ought to be a good, well-labeled, rapidly changing exhibition of books every day of the year in every library in the land, so that books young and old, fine and not-so-fine, in public and institutional collections could

enlarge and refresh their circle of admirers and friends. Publicists, outreach librarians, and other social workers of the book trade would probably say it is good for their character – and for ours.

Something else can be said for carefully mounted exhibitions of fine books. It is that other things can be shown with them – things that are part of the lives of printers and part of the life of a well-made book but that most readers are rarely privileged to see. These hidden elements include such things as type, leads, furniture and chases, woodblocks and engravings, manuscripts, galleys and page proofs, correspondence between author and printer, design sketches and tests, trial pages, ink and paper samples, trial covers and bindings. A serious printer's studio is a laboratory where fascinating experiments in the making of cultural history are constantly underway.

In this particular instance, we have a closely focused show of selected works by five mature, accomplished California fine presses: Ninja Press, Peter Rutledge Koch, Turkey Press, Moving Parts Press, and Foolscap Press. Two of these presses are joint ventures, so we are looking at the work of seven artist printers altogether: Carolee Campbell, Peter Koch, Harry and Sandra Reese, Felicia Rice, Lawrence G. Van Velzer, and Peggy Gotthold. All are significant figures in the long generation that follows Everson, Stauffacher, Wilson, and Hoyem. There are some very interesting tutorial and material links between the seven printers here on show and those who have preceded them, but I like to think it is the spiritual connections that matter most. These don't always follow the pedagogical or corporeal line of descent.

No less important than the connections are the disconnections. Each of these five presses is plainly different from the others; each is also different from all that have gone before. Indeed, there is a watershed distinction between these five presses and the many that preceded them. Every printer in this show is deeply familiar with the meditative pleasures of handsetting metal type, but each has also lived some decades into the digital age and felt the changes it is bringing.

I will hazard a guess that each of these printers holds fast to the old technology for at least two reasons. First, deployed with skill and care, it gives impeccable material results. Second, it unites the worker and the work, artisan and artifact, in ways that easier, faster, more "efficient" and impersonal means cannot. But these are also printers who have looked for ways to bend the new technologies into the moral orbit of the old – and each can teach us something about how this might be done.

Most (not all) of the great foundry types are of European origin, and European foundries suffered heavily in the Second World War. Those that managed to recapitalize and retool promptly started to lose ground, like their North American counterparts, to the hot-metal keyboard machines (Monotype and Linotype primarily). Then the foundries and the hot-metal machine manufacturers struggled together against the photosetting machines. Then every last photosetting machine, and all but a tiny, barricaded remnant of the world of metal type, was washed quite suddenly away, replaced by weightless, intangible digital type set on almost weightless personal computers. The last new Linotype machine was built in 1976, the last new Monotype in 1987. The last major European typefoundry closed in 1990, while the last in the USA lingered on in a kind of coma until 1993. These events have occurred in the working lifetimes of the printers in this show.

Metal type is still being cast from old matrices, in a few working museums and privately owned boutique operations. Newly designed metal faces are also – on rare occasions, at enormous cost – still being cut and struck and cast for setting by hand. Hundreds of working Monotype and Linotype machines are being maintained by devotees around the world. But if printing is an art instead of an antiquarian pastime, it cannot rely entirely on leftovers.

Digital type, by contrast, is one of the slipperiest, most unlocalized of commodities. Like a pop tune, a digital font can sprout in Berlin or Los Angeles one day and reappear in identical form a day later in Dar es Salaam, Reykjavík, Kansas City and Seoul. Good typographers can do fine things with such type, and an enormous amount of knowledge, care and intelligence can be woven into the font itself by its maker. Yet as an article of commerce, it is just an intangible slurry of digital code, transportable instantly and at no discernible cost from one hemisphere to another. Like money and internet gossip, it seems as a rule to have no *terroir*. And it is hard to believe it can really change hands or do meaningful work when it cannot be cradled or touched with the hand to begin with.

This is not quite how it seemed when the revolution began. Digital type has existed after a fashion since the 1960s, but in the early days its only virtue was speed. (It was useful for setting such things as telephone directories, from mountains of data stored on magnetic tape.) In its now-familiar, fluent and scalable form, it erupted rather suddenly, in the 1980s, from the southern tip of San Francisco Bay. Two mathematicians, John Warnock and Charles Geschke, working in and near Palo Alto, developed a flexible, elegant method of describing complex, nested and discontinuous two-dimensional shapes – pages full of letterforms, for instance. This essentially mathematical achievement took the outward form of a concatenative programming language known as PostScript, which was for several years the one and only product of Adobe Systems, a company founded by Warnock and Geschke in 1982. By the end of the decade, both the business of typesetting and the culture of type design had been radically transformed by this language no one ever spoke or heard. Publishing, by 1990, had become a ubiquitous desktop activity. Monotype, Linotype and other major firms had converted their accumulated wealth of metal and phototype faces to a form that would run on the personal computer, and anyone who wished to could compete with them on almost equal terms from a half-furnished basement room.

People in the fine press world watched these events with interest and bemusement. Their sources of foundry type had rapidly dwindled away. Revivals of those types, along with new designs, were suddenly appearing left and right, but only in digital form – and digital type, when it comes out of the computer, is two-dimensional. This is good for photo-offset printing, but letterpress printers are sculptors. They think and work in three dimensions, not in two. And letterpress is an intrinsically limited medium, while photo-offset is not. Printing a book by letterpress is like undertaking a climbing expedition. A lot of organization and preparation leads to a lot of physical labor, which has to be finished with finite supplies in a finite time and culminates, with luck, in a partly tangible, partly spiritual reward. Printing a book by photo-offset is a great deal more like taking a trip by car. It involves a lot of packing and unpacking, interspersed with motorized noise, but when supplies run out, you just buy more and, if you choose to, keep on going.

In the 1980s, most of the people involved with digital type thought letterpress archaic and had very little interest in scribal or typographic tradition. Equally, most real typographers and calligraphers knew nothing about computer engineering. But there were a few well-placed exceptions. One was Charles Bigelow; another was Sumner Stone. Bigelow, who had studied with Stauffacher and with Hermann Zapf, was typography editor at *Fine Print* from 1980 to 1990 and taught digital typography at Stanford from 1982 to 1995. For a year, while the firm was still in its infancy, he also served part-time as typographic advisor to Adobe Systems. Stone, a mathematician and calligrapher, became Adobe's first full-time Director of Typography in 1984. Like Stanley Morison at the Monotype Corporation sixty years earlier, he launched an ambitious program on three fronts. One (shared with the new digital arms of Monotype and Linotype) involved the conversion of existing faces to digital form. Another involved the creation of new typefaces suited to serious reading. The third was an educational program, aimed at creating a market for well-made fonts at a time when most commercial designers had lost touch with typographic values. As part of this enterprise, Stone began supplying desktop computers and fonts to Stauffacher and other fine letterpress printers in the San Francisco area. Bigelow, for his part, ensured that digital type design was well represented in the pages of *Fine Print,* along with more traditional typographic topics.

Many fine printers do some design work for the trade and academic press. Stone was right to think they would also make instructive demands on the digital typefounders and would set a useful example for designers who lacked their expertise. Still it was not clear how even the best digital type could be of much use in making *fine* books. However good it got, it was still flat. Two-dimensional artwork can be turned into three dimensions by photo-etching a slab of zinc or magnesium, but this is a costly and caustic industrial process – plausible for a title page or a handful of illustrations, but not for a hundred pages of text.

The answer to this conundrum came from left field. Most of us who have worked in typography for any length of time, no matter how strictly we focus on books and on serious literature, have also designed at least one plastic shopping bag and a shipping carton or two. Ignominious objects like this, which involve putting small bits of text on unruly substrates, are printed on rotary presses with flexible plates and cheap, low-viscosity inks. In the early 1990s, letterpress printers began to notice that the new photopolymer plates used in this process might have a more appealing application. The plates are easily made, by exposing a soft photopolymer blank to ultraviolet light through a photographic negative. This hardens the exposed parts of the plate, and the softer, unexposed parts are washed out with plain water. The result looks and feels like molded plastic, unworthy to share the imposing stone with so regal a substance as typemetal. But a well-made photopolymer plate has a crisp, firm printing surface. It is easy to mount type-high and lock up in the press, and it will print like a good woodcut.[18]

A flimsy tin-and-plastic electrified cakebox, the photopolymer platemaker, now sits somewhere in the corner of many illustrious pressrooms, looking just as out-of-place as the photocopier and fax machine near the thousand-pound handpresses, the typecases and lead racks. But that cakebox is the link between the letterpress and the computer. The unattractive sheets of sleek, eroded plastic it produces are in fact the magic carpets bearing disembodied digital type back into three-dimensional reality, where the voice of literature has substance, not just form.

There are fleas in every carpet. The typographical obscenities committed hourly on computers around the world – emaciated and ill-spaced fake small capitals, typewriter-keyboard dumb quotes and vertical apostrophes, hyphens in place of em dashes and en dashes, letterspaced italic, clumsily forged diacritics, childish parodies of type design, and other symptoms of cultural ill-health – can now be given three-dimensional standing. All the indignities that can be visited on letterforms by powerful image-manipulation software can be translated to the letterpress as well.

But letterpress artists themselves, and not just vandals, clowns and unsupervised children, have found uses for these tricks. Photopolymer has also allowed fine printers to gorge themselves, if they wish, on line drawings and other illustrations, making the letterpress page more cinematic than ever before. It has also given fine printers the option of translating manuscript directly into letterpress, avoiding type altogether, or mixing type and handwriting, or made and found letterforms and images, in any proportions they please. New links are being forged between the graphic and the glyphic, the written and the sculpted. What began as a baling-wire-and-chewing-gum fix for the problem of the disembodied type font has in some respects brought letterpress back to good health, and in other respects has transformed it into something it has never been before.

VI

The seven printers in this show can speak for themselves better by far than I could speak on their behalf, and it seems to me the work they make can speak more eloquently yet. They have each devoted their lives, or a large part of their lives, to the making of fine books – and lives, after a while, get to be complicated things, never altogether free of time and place but never completely absorbed in them either. Some of us at least find that work can at times attain a kind of clarity that life – especially an artisan's life – does not.

Carolee Campbell of Los Angeles was born just a year after Andrew Hoyem, but she was busy for many years with things besides printing. Her first career was in the theater, her second

in photography. She studied letterpress with Harry and Sandra Reese, who are a decade younger than she, and established her own imprint, Ninja Press, in 1984. In one respect at least, she is the most conservative printer in the show. She has never used anything but handset metal type in any of her books, though she has used polymer plates for illustrations and analphabetic symbols. In other regards, she is one of the most creative and adventurous printers I know. In her mature work, nothing is done in the familiar, easy way. The binding structures and illustration techniques never repeat; the papers and other materials are always a new challenge; so is the typographic design. But she is hardly without interest in the past. Two important pieces of equipment in her pressroom, a galley cabinet and proof press, come from the Plantin Press of Saul and Lillian Marks. She has no direct connection with Ward Ritchie, and still less with Ritchie's teacher, François-Louis Schmied, but I think that she and Schmied have something important in common: something theatrical, in the best sense of the word. In their luminous and concentrated pages, as in a good performance of a play, things appear *just to happen,* yet they are always perfectly timed.

One of my favorites among her books is her edition of W.S. Merwin's long poem *The Real World of Manuel Córdova,* finished in 1995. It is a poem about a river, printed as a river, so it becomes the map of a river, on paper that ripples like a river and is as richly colored as water gorged with red Amazonian mud. It is a river of words and a map of the mind, but it is also, first and last, a book, and so the sheet, 15 feet long, folds into something as compact as a Javanese or Tibetan sutra.

Peter Rutledge Koch, who is now the reigning master among the master printers of Berkeley, was born in Missoula in 1943. He was raised in Montana, fly-fishing for trout, which is a fine way to learn how time unfolds and how lean and subtle elements tend by nature to arrange themselves in seemingly empty space – two things that printers need to know. A devotion to those frontier philosophers called the Presocratics is one of the many things that Peter and I share, and no printer since Robert Estienne in the sixteenth century has done as much as he on their behalf. He is the only North American printer who has ever, in 370 years, commissioned a new Greek typeface to be cut by hand in steel and cast for handsetting, and the only printer anywhere on the planet who has done this in our time. Like his teacher Adrian Wilson, he has a broad range, from the abstemious to the hilarious. Like Lewis and Dorothy Allen half a century ago, he has also made a point of carrying printing with him in his travels, not leaving it at home. (He printed Joseph Brodsky's *Watermark* in Venice in 2006.) For him as for Wilson, Stauffacher and Everson, printing is a brotherhood, a calling, and a constant celebration as well as a sacred craft.

Koch has made considerable use of digital type as well as handset metal, and of the latest, high-tech means of two-dimensional color printing and imaging. He feels, I think, an ongoing obligation to bring the historical and the contemporary bluntly face to face and let them stare each other down. The outsized, ghostly images in Deborah Magpie Earling's *Sacajewea,* for example, lead abruptly from the Old West of buffalo slaughter and teepees to the New: a tangle of freeways on the banks of the Columbia. The old-looking type in *Sacajewea* is likewise genuinely old and at the same time genuinely new. It is seventeenth-century Dutch, quite haphazardly cast. A certain sharp Dutch merchant must have been very pleased to sell it, about 1671, to the visiting English clergyman who took it back to Oxford. But the font Koch employs is Jonathan Hoefler's faithful digital replica of the seventeenth-century metal. The text was set on a computer and the type restored to three dimensions only when the book was ready for printing.

Harry and Sandra Reese, who publish under the imprints Turkey Press and Edition Reese, have a habit of saying they belong to no tradition. This is in fact a quite traditional American thing to say – and in saying it, they know, of course, that history is harder than that to escape, especially for printers. In truth, they belong to multiple traditions and seem happy to be caught in the act of slipping from one to another. When it pleases them to do so, they participate in the high church rituals of perfectionist typography,

making gracious two-page spreads that would have gladdened the heart of Adrian Wilson. (Their 2007 edition of *The Sea Gazer* by Michael Hannon – clearly one of their favorite poets – is that kind of book.) When they choose, they also dress down and go slumming. The typewriter keyboard quotation marks, missed ligatures and haphazardly mixed species of numerals in *33⅓ Off the Record,* for example, are plainly meant to say that they reserve the right to amuse themselves and refuse to be indentured to any one aesthetic. They share with Ward Ritchie not only an affection for Southern California but also a love of pranks, jokes, and rich, sensuous color. A printer they more openly admire is the late Dick Higgins, a participant in the Fluxus enterprise and for some years proprietor of a wacky but resolute venture called Something Else Press, begun in New York City in 1963. Higgins studied with the patron saint of Fluxus, John Cage, who may in fact have passed along a lesson or two learned earlier from Ritchie's erstwhile partner, the earnest and un-Fluxus-like Gregg Anderson.

Generally speaking, Fluxus artists were far more interested in *doing* art than in *making* it. The Reeses make objects rather than staging events, but books are not quite ordinary objects, and many of the Reeses' books are even more event-like than the books of other printers. They are also sometimes confrontational, in the friendly California sort of way. The Reeses are, for example, happy to package a poem called *The Standard* in a binding that looks like a bar of gold, somehow subtracted from Fort Knox. And since that poem, thumbing its nose at the idea of money, proposes dead rats as a standard of value, the Reeses are also happy to include, inside that classy gold-bar binding, like a frontispiece, a genuine Victor rat trap.

Felicia Rice, of Moving Parts Press, studied with both Stauffacher and Everson when they were teaching at Santa Cruz, and later worked with Adrian Wilson in San Francisco. She also worked at length with Sherwood Grover, a former Grabhorn pressman and proprietor of the Grace Hoper Press, whose equipment she now owns. She has printed books as classically restrained and quietly lovely as any by her teachers. (A favorite of mine is her edition of

Francisco Alarcón's *De Amor oscuro,* issued in 1991.) In 1998, she leapt to the other extreme with the cinematic, hypertextual and hyperenergetic *Codex Espangliensis.*[19] Classical typography rests on the assumption that boundaries are good and useful things – not sacred, not immutable, but useful: so useful that order, life and beauty cannot survive without them. This codex – an accordion-folded stream-of-unconsciousness collage by Enrique Chagoya with raw-edged chunks of highly literate and frequently hilarious graffiti by Guillermo Gómez-Peña – explores a world in which boundaries have turned into border fences and homelands into jails and refugee camps. (Gómez-Peña, not surprisingly, is another artist sympathetic to the lingering ghost of Fluxus.)

In the twelve years since *Codex Espangliensis,* Rice has challenged traditional printerly values and typographic practice in several other ways, combining book art with folk art, typography with cloth, and investigating the degree to which a book might be a kind of incompletely grown-up toybox full of dissonant cultural echoes. She has also continued to make conventional books of a handsomely unconventional kind. The obvious example is *Cosmogonie intime,* completed in 2005. This is a group of poems by Yves Peyré, threaded on a long spine of colorful but spare and bony drawings made by the San Francisco artist Ray Rice, who died before the book was published. He was Felicia Rice's father.

Lawrence Van Velzer, like William Everson, is a printer's son and has known the craft since he was a child. He and his partner Peggy Gotthold both worked for years at the Arion Press under Andrew Hoyem, and both are highly skilled – but Gotthold is the only one among the seven printers in this show who was trained first and foremost as a binder. While she has bound books for many fine presses, the most inventive of her structures and containers seem to be those she has done for her own and Van Velzer's Foolscap Press. It also matters, I think, that Van Velzer and Gotthold are skilled puppeteers. Their books are theatrical in quite a different sense than Carolee Campbell's or some of the Reeses' or Rice's, and the difference lies in part in a sense of scale. Foolscap Press books are no smaller, and the texts no shorter, than those of other fine printers, nor is the type more diminutive in size; but Foolscap books are frequently constructed in such a way as to draw the reader into a miniature world, as a puppet theater does. Van Velzer and Gotthold are, accordingly, fond of fables and folktales, of books that are nested inside other books, and of illustrations involving optical illusion and distortion.

Unusually among fine printers, especially in California, they have made a point of *not* publishing poetry. (They have never, so far as I know, made any formal commitment not to do so; I think they have found, quite simply, that poetry as usually practiced tends to hamper rather than feed their particular kind of imagination.) They have worked their magic with texts by some of the finest fabulists on record – Ursula Le Guin and Stephen Leacock, for example – but have also often chosen to write their books themselves. This adds to another illusion, possibly central to their work: that the text has grown from seed in the small theater of its binding. Printers more often see their project the other way round, and therefore court the illusion that the binding has grown like bark and leaves to clothe and flesh out the text that a writer has written.

VII

The late John Russell, an articulate critic of art in all its forms, said of the painter Piet Mondrian that "his subject matter was the workings of the universe, not the workings of his own temperament."[20] Whatever an artist's subjects may be, or whatever he may think they are, the workings of the universe are the subject of art itself, which has no individual human temperament to be troubled or misled by. That is why artists make such efforts to allow their art to practice itself rather than telling it what to do. But in a culture that values nothing above the self, the artist's temperament is likely to loom large. This is not an entirely hopeless state of affairs, but it is not much of a window through which to view the universe.

"Time is the soul of space," writes W.J.T. Mitchell, and "literature, like consciousness itself, is a complex structure with multiple dimensions."[21] There, in brief, is the rationale behind Adrian Wilson's aim of provoking people to "read less better, instead of more faster." The printed book is our basic means of giving literature an independent existence. It is one of our few basic means of giving the same gift to consciousness. The book is a kind of house – not quite for reality itself, but for our knowledge and impressions of reality – to live in. It may look like nothing much – just a roll or stack of paper – but a book, if it is a repository of literature and consciousness, will prove to be a similarly complex, multidimensional structure. We are always looking, when we read, for the structure and the texture of the text, because these are indispensable and integral to meaning. We often don't look *consciously* for structure and texture as we read, but we are looking even so. Good typographers and printers help us find them.

Trade books and fine books alike have changed since the 1830s, and since the Second World War, and even since the 1980s. In the world of trade publishing, it is easy enough to see that some of the changes have been for the better, others for the worse. In the world of fine printing, where serious and conscious experimentation (as well as conservation) is constantly going on, it is harder to say how fruitful or unfruitful any particular move may be – and often, perhaps, it is better not to say. The art of printing, like any living art, is an ecology, constantly testing itself and feeling its way along, pursuing what seems to work and dropping what seems not to. Artists are driven by visions, not by moral judgments or critical pronouncements. But the art itself is not driven by any of these things. It is driven just by being what it is, and is therefore working blind.

The sense of touch is crucial to the blind. And there is something elemental that nearly all printers and publishers have until recently had in common: namely a fondness for tangible things: an affection for things you can touch and hang on to or hand to a friend, and for things you can turn your back on or put on a shelf and return to, a day or a week or a century later,

to discover they're still there, still full of things that someone knew, still full of things they might yet show and tell you. The things printers make are *things full of things*: tangible congeries of intangibles: *piñatas* that needn't be broken because they will endlessly open and close, reenacting with every turn of the page the continuous, illuminating puzzle of the real. Printing, for this reason, has been very different from broadcasting. It has turned language into a physical fact, independently present in space and in time. The printed word is a thing you can stub your eye or your toe on, like a coconut, like a stone.

This is now changing. The type with which books are printed was effectively vaporized twenty-five years ago. It was flung into the digital melting pot, from which only its ghostly and rubbery shape would return. A decade later, a small and wholly disorganized band of fine printers, with slender resources, seized their chance and brought those letterforms back, as best they could, to material being. It was important to them that letters be physically real. But that was just a raid, in the context of a global revolution. The disincarnation of type was fundamentally successful and relatively thorough. Most readers currently alive have never touched or seen a letterpress book.

The book itself, not just the type in which it is set, is dematerializing now. In fact the book has been shuffling off its durable but not immortal coil, slipping away from robust physical existence, for two centuries or more. The first step was the rationalization and dramatization of letterforms in the Neoclassical and Romantic age, which severed the anatomical relation between manuscript and print. Then came the drift from natural rag paper to brittle, acidic substitutes, through industrial reliance on groundwood and bleach. Then the shift from the sculptural fact of letterpress to the flat simulation of high-speed offset printing, and the move from cases and sewn bindings to shiny paper covers and glue. The latest step is of course the shift from ink on paper to scrolling text on handheld digital displays.

Fine work can be done, and has been done, in fugitive media, and I do not doubt that good typography will find its way into the e-book (where at present it is pretty much unknown). Nor do I doubt that e-books will prove useful. But letters that come and go on the screen are never the same as the ones you can hold in your hand. Not even the eye and the mind can touch those fugitive shapes in the way they can touch a material thing.

As the physical book evaporates from the world of common experience, there are signs that the love of the book, and warm, hard patronage for the costly art of the book, are dematerializing too. The Zamorano Club, a bibliophilic organization founded in Los Angeles in 1927, put its impressive book collection into storage in 1991 and auctioned it off in 1999. The Rounce & Coffin Club, another such organization founded in 1931, folded completely in 2005. Other such groups – the Book Club of California chief among them – are still decidedly alive but not without their episodes of self-doubt and vocational confusion. To be sure, there are still collectors. Some of the fortunes made in Silicon Valley through developing the technology of the electronic book have already been spent in part on fine collections of real books. But librarians – meaning a few alert, well-positioned, courageous librarians – have increasingly become the patrons of record on a disinterested public's behalf.

At the same time, side by side with the art of the book, we have what are lately called "book arts." Independent centers and galleries now celebrate and exhibit them, and universities teach them. Peter Koch has described very well what this typically involves:

The book arts ... are easier to teach than historical connoisseurship and fine printing, and ... they are more fun and oriented toward personal expression.... We are now accustomed to seeing the imaginative use of materials like maxi-pads, banana wrappers, fortune cookies, dim-sum boxes, coat-hangers, and used cigarette packages. This flourishing is augmented by novel book bindings in the shape of toilet seats and shower caps.... These wild things have been welcomed by curators and art critics and are proclaimed artists' books.[22]

The book itself – the elusive, intangible book that writers and printers continue to dream of – is still vigorous. Great books are being written; great type is being cut and set; great printed books are also being made. But our society's relation to the book now seems to me increasingly unhealthy and unlikely to survive in its present form. Under these conditions, I believe that the artist printers among us, like those of the Renaissance and those of our recent past, are performing an invaluable service. Their experiments, I think, are a vital form of research, and their achievements, at their best, a form of art we should hold dear. However uncomfortable books may be in the art museum's locked glass cases, I am glad that once in a while we find them there. I like to think they might forgive us the discomfort if we promise to keep thinking.

AUTHOR NOTE

Robert Bringhurst was born in Los Angeles in 1946. He lives now in *Altissima California* – on a small island off the British Columbia coast. From 1986 to 1990 he was contributing editor of the legendary San Francisco journal *Fine Print: A Review for the Arts of the Book*. His own books on typographic subjects include *The Elements of Typographic Style* (now in its third edition), *A Short History of the Printed Word* (revised edition, co-authored with Warren Chappell), *The Solid Form of Language* (2004) and *The Surface of Meaning: Books & Book Design in Canada* (2008).

For the works appearing in the notes below, full citations are given in the Further Reading section at the end of the book.

1 Cook et al. 1884 is the catalogue of the exhibition.

2 Bosqui's *Memoirs,* published in 1904, run to 280 pages, but they make only the briefest mention of the printing firm he owned for fifty years and do not say a word about the individual books he produced. A good summary of his life can be found in David Karel's *Dictionnaire des artistes de langue française en Amérique du Nord* (Québec: Musée du Québec / Presses de l'Université Laval, 1992): 101–3.

3 Updike's research assistant during his final years at Harvard was George Laban Harding (1893–1976), a native of Indiana who later moved to San Francisco. Twelve years before his death, Harding's excellent personal library on the history of printing passed into the hands of the California Historical Society, becoming part of their invaluable Kemble Collection. The enormous archive amassed by Taylor & Taylor is now part of the Kemble Collection as well.

4 From a conversation with Ruth Teiser: Robert Grabhorn 1968: 99.

5 Also in conversation with Ruth Teiser: Edwin Grabhorn 1968: 77.

6 Quoted in Baughman 1966: 40.

7 Johnston 1979: 1.

8 Edwin Grabhorn 1933, quoted in Blumenthal 1977: 119f.

9 Many fanciful things have been said about the term *Parmelian.* Adams wanted to believe it was derived from Greek μέλας, meaning black. Parmelia, however, is a genus of foliose lichens, named in 1803 by Erik Acharius. It was Acharius who coined the term, and he derived it from Greek πάρμη, meaning a buckler or small shield. The word soon leaked from botany into popular culture, redeployed as a name for women, ships, at least one town, and several country estates. Once Parmelia was adopted as a woman's name, false etymologies based on Greek μέλι, meaning honey, began to crop up (and have lately sprouted like weeds on the internet). Do Adams's photos resemble shields or foliose lichens? Not especially. But Ms Moore appears to have chosen the word precisely because she *didn't* know what it meant.

10 Adams's delightfully unvarnished account of the making of *Taos Pueblo* is in Adams 1978: 74f, 175f, 187f. Bentley's account of the making of *Sierra Nevada* is in Bentley 1941. A facsimile edition of *Taos Pueblo* (with letterpress work by Lawton and Alfred Kennedy, and the images reproduced by gravure) was published in 1977, but it is now almost as scarce as the first edition. The 2006 trade reissue of *Sierra Nevada* (with its fatuous colophon and fraudulent dedication) is easy to find but gives no sense of the 1938 original.

11 These were all commissioned works, produced between 1942 and 1948. They were printed by the Plantin Press but bore the imprint *Privatdruck der Pazifischen Presse.* Not surprisingly, Pazifische Presse was itself an expatriate creation, founded in Los Angeles by Felix Guggenheim and Ernst Gottlieb.

12 *Novum Psalterium,* the great edition of the Latin psalms that Everson printed (but did not himself publish) is sometimes credited to "St. Albert's Press." That is actually the name of the printing facility in St. Albert's Priory, Oakland, where, as Brother Antoninus, Everson kept his press and printed what he published under the Albertus Magnus imprint. The psalter, made up from Everson's sheets, was actually published by Estelle Doheny in Los Angeles.

13 Wilson 1990: 173.

14 Wilson 1990: 186–7. (To put this in perspective, it may help

to know that Jack was 28 years old and Adrian 24. Sperisen, the old man of the tale, was 39.)

15 Haselwood published a few more books using his own name as an imprint, then went on to other things. He is now Joko Haselwood, a Buddhist priest in the Soto Zen lineage, leading the Empty Bowl Sangha in Cotati, California.

16 Another valuable summary of the work of these four printers exists in the form of an exhibition catalogue, written by Sandra Kirshenbaum for a show at UC Davis, entitled *Five Fine Printers* (1979). The fifth of the group was Richard Bigus, a California native who had studied with Stauffacher and Everson at UC Santa Cruz and started to publish under the imprint Labyrinth Editions. He was very young (younger, in fact, than five of the seven printers in the present show), but he had done fine and innovative work. Soon after the Davis exhibition, however, Bigus left California for an unsettled teaching career, moving briskly through universities in Ohio, Iowa, New Zealand, and Nebraska, before settling in Hawaii. Between 1978 and 1989, he also conducted a raucous public debate with several unappreciative critics in the pages of *Fine Print*. Toward the end of this time, his letterpress output dwindled away. For the details, see *Fine Print* 4.1: 15; 4.3: 80; 4.4: 106; 5.2: 50–51; 5.3: 84–85; 7.1: 18–19; 9.3: 117–119; 10.3: 91–93; 11.3: 164–165; 15.2: 62.

17 Other good and useful journals have set themselves some different but related tasks and succeeded in filling their own shoes. One of these journals is *Matrix* (not the feminist annual formerly published in Los Angeles nor the literary quarterly published now in Montreal but the typographic annual founded in England by John and Rose Randle in 1981). Another is *Parenthesis* (a peripatetic semiannual founded in 1998 by the Fine Press Book Association).

18 Someone must have been first to make this experiment, and I am sorry I do not know who it was. Patrick Reagh of Sebastopol and Gerald Lange of Los Angeles were certainly among the pioneers, and in 1998 Lange published a useful little book on the subject.

19 Californians will not need to be told what *Spanglish* means – any more than Édouard Bosqui of Montréal would have needed to be told the definition of *Franglais*. Habitués of Stanford will likewise recognize that *espangliensis* is the *nomen adiectiuum loci,* or locative adjective, formed from Spanglish – implying that Spanglish must be the name of a placeless place as well as its hybrid language. Just as the *Codex Oxoniensis* is the book that belongs to (i.e., has been taken to) Oxford, so the *Codex Espangliensis* is the book that belongs to (or ought to be taken to) wherever Spanglish is spoken.

20 John Russell, *The Meanings of Modern Art* (New York: MOMA / Harper & Row, 1981): 227.

21 These remarks occur in a well-known essay, "Spatial Form in Literature," first published in 1980 in the journal *Critical Inquiry*. It is reprinted in *The Language of Images*, a collection of essays also edited by Mitchell, published by the University of Chicago Press in the same year.

22 Koch 2010b: 36.

The Art of the Book in California: Five Contemporary Presses

PETER RUTLEDGE KOCH

I am tempted to hang my introductory statement to this exhibition of five exemplary California presses upon the words of William Everson, poet and printer, who when inaugurating his Equinox Press in Berkeley back in 1947 stated, "As a creative man, the richest thing I can do is to write a poem, and the next is to print it."[1]

I say "tempted" because as with any grouping of mavericks — artists, poets, rock musicians, and printers especially — no two are in agreement and at least one in five will eschew poetry entirely or claim no ancestors other than those *not* named or listed below. And not all of us will readily believe the claim that printing is a fine art, and that the book indeed can be a work of art even when it is made under the same conditions as a painting or a poem.

Yet the conditions are such that broad and sweeping statements concerning art and the western *Zeitgeist* and its confrontation with the great Pacific Ocean are apt. Everson traces in his extended essay *Archetype West*[2] the development of his own poet-craft forward from Ancient Greek and Buddhist sources through to the San Francisco Renaissance and the subsequent Beat movements all colliding in the dramatic and elemental California landscape that limns a climacteric of western art and culture. He defines a distinct California literary and cultural aesthetic that flows from the West back towards the East, to the old worlds of New England and Europe; and west to Japan, China, and beyond. Everson's contention is that California artists are far less tradition-bound and conventional than their eastern counterparts. He delineates the Hegelian progression of western art and culture as a frontier spirit — a wild and westward-moving spirit — terminating on the Pacific Coast, and there confronting older Asian philosophies of religion and art. If the thesis is arguable, it is nonetheless compelling when we consider California's impact since the Second World War.

California has a distinctive presence in the book arts on the international scene, just as it has in all other cultural fields, from literature and cinema to painting. California is west of the West.[3]

Here an arresting natural landscape is the setting for the collision and commingling of cultures on a scale and at a speed that has never been seen before. Within two hundred years the Native American cultures have been decimated, the Spanish Mission culture of Alta California which succeeded those cultures has been destroyed, while emigrants from Europe (via Canada, the eastern United States, and directly from Europe), from Africa (via the American South and the Caribbean), from Latin America, and from all Asia have flooded to swell us to a population of over thirty-seven million, thirty million of whom arrived here from elsewhere in the last 70 years.

The books in this exhibition deeply reflect this tumultuous environment of cultural influences.

Parallel with the world of the poets and artists of San Francisco and the Pacific Coast south to Los Angeles there is the culture of the printing press where printer/publishers by their own art significantly contribute to our material culture as collaborators in the art forms and artifacts that issue from their presses.

For Everson, both poet and printer, the literary frontier in California was first illumined by Brett Hart, Mark Twain, and Jack London — all of whom were deeply influenced by the magnificent landscapes of the Sierra Nevada and the Pacific Coast. In the aftermath of the Gold Rush the Bohemian coast from San Francisco south to Big Sur swelled with writers, the more renowned of whom were Robinson Jeffers, Frank Norris, Janet Lewis, Ambrose Bierce, and Henry Miller. These writers and their followers counted many printers among their friends. The Grabhorn Press, Jane Grabhorn's Jumbo and Colt Presses and the young Jack Stauffacher's

Greenwood Press stood out prominently at the center of the San Francisco art scene. From the San Francisco Renaissance and the Beat movement through to the emergence of the hippies, writers Kenneth Rexroth, Robert Duncan, Gary Snyder, Richard Brautigan, Philip Lamantia, Lawrence Ferlinghetti, Michael McClure, Charles Bukowski, and others collaborated with visual artists to produce limited editions and press books that still inspire young poets and artists today. Literary printers William Everson, David Hazelwood, Adrian Wilson, Andrew Hoyem, Graham Macintosh, and Clifford Burke were deeply involved.

Because it is in the medium of print that the writer's craft finds itself visible, the spirit that drives the typographer and master printer is that same spirit that moves the artist and writer – a spirit that moves thoughtfully, acknowledging traditions, breaking rules, experimenting, discovering new materials, and finding new expressions to substantiate one's vision.

The purpose of this exhibition is to substantiate the claim that California printers are at the center of a deep artistic experiment, relentlessly pushing the frontiers of art in the form of their printed books.

In an essay entitled "The Book as Object," Michel Butor provocatively stated that "every honest writer today is confronted by the *problem of the book*." Butor asked, "Why are we satisfied by the book?" His question can be restated more elaborately as: Since we can "freeze" what we say, sing or visualize in a considerable number of mediums, ranging from carved stone to digital capture, why exactly are we so attached to the book? Butor answered his own question thus: "The sole, but significant, superiority not only of books but of all writing over the means of direct recording, which is incomparably more accurate, is the simultaneous exposure to our eyes of what our ears can grasp only sequentially. The development of the book's form . . . has always been oriented toward a greater emphasis of this feature."[4]

In a slightly different context we can read an equally provocative statement by the poet and printer William Everson, in an essay entitled "The Poem as Icon." About the book itself, Everson wrote that "whatever you do with a book, you are working with it also as a symbol. It is the implication and consequences that inhere in the book as a symbol that makes both the incentive, and also the terrible warp in your judgment as you approach it. There are very few perfect books."[5]

Beyond these two reflections, beyond tool and icon, there lies the complex concept of *the book as a work of art*.

Over the last forty years a major paradigm shift has slowly occurred in the conception and production of the book as art and artifact. Traditionally, books considered as works of art were defined either as books *containing* original prints (the early-twentieth-century art-historical model of the *livre d'artiste*) published by a patron/connoisseur, or as *fine printing*, which California bibliophiles James D. Hart and Ward Ritchie understood to mean typographically sophisticated and handsomely illustrated books suitable for a gentleman's library – books produced by the Limited Editions Club, for example.

All this changed by the late 1970s, when a more critical and sophisticated approach to a book's conceptual, physical, and formal properties required more of it than ever before as a work of art — no longer would books with art *in* them be enough. The book began to acquire layers of meaning previously regarded by readers as unrelated to the content: both the social context of book production and the physical structure and materials of the book became signatures of the artist/printer as book-producer, and more reflective of the meaning of the book's contents.

This change of paradigm - a more inclusive idea of what constitutes a work of art, coupled with a deepening concept of the book as object - has matured greatly in the last twenty years. The complexities of craft and knowledge that coexist in the making of a handmade book today encourage collaboration - younger artists, printers, and writers are now joined, influenced, and informed by conservation bookbinders, artisanal papermakers, type designers, digital media engineers, and contemporary scholarship in the history of the book. Finally, and quite importantly, book-producers have become more highly aware of the inventions (and conventions) of contemporary art in other media, with its accompanying overburden of concepts and contextualizations.

The art of the book has indeed matured into an art form that exceeds all former standards for the book as object, and it is in California that a considerable number of exemplars have been made in the last fifty years. This fact has been only partially documented and while the books are often represented in major worldwide collections, exhibitions, and catalogue publications, no definitive bibliography exists to guide us: we are all pioneers in the field.

Artists' books became a separate genre in the 1960s and 1970s when there was a flourishing of intentionally cheap artist-produced and self-published books. Exemplified by Ed Ruscha's brilliant but ultimately cynical exercise in banality, *Twenty-Six Gasoline Stations*, the movement united mass-market production values with elitist content aimed at, and driven by, the academic and museum-conscious art-class. That "democratic multiple" concept reached its peak in the late 1970s. These books are documented and examined in detail by, among others, Clive Phillpot[7] and Johanna Drucker.[8]

In contradistinction to small-press independent publishing that mocked and deliberately subverted mass-market publishing that flourished in the 1960s and 1970s art world, we begin to see by 1975 an entirely new concept of the book as artifact. Younger artists grew tired of working in cheap and often uninspired alternative-press production and found that the discipline and dedication of master-craftsmanship revived an enduring sense of appropriateness and integrity that was too obviously missing in the more cynical and frenzied mass-market pop-art environment of the sixties. In northern California, the generation of artists and writers mentored by highly literate elder printer/publishers such as William Everson, Jack Stauffacher, and Adrian Wilson, began to see virtue in historically-informed design practices, fine printing, hand made papers, and sophisticated and original typographic styles.[9] At the same time, they were continually exposed to the more adventuresome works published by the Auerhahn Press and City Lights Books in San Francisco and Black Sparrow Press in Los Angeles — a heady brew indeed.

Significantly, it was in 1975 that *Fine Print: The Review for the Arts of the Book* was founded in San Francisco. It is in the pages of this journal that we first see documentation of the rising generation of art-minded printers. With their support, and also with enthusiastic editorial support from publishers and curators, *Fine Print* soon became *the* international journal and *the* leader in the field of the book arts. That same year (1975) saw the publication of Jack Stauffacher's *Phaedrus* and William Everson's *Granite and Cypress* — the twin icons of the new movement.

In 1979 the Library Associates of the University of California, Davis, mounted an exhibition entitled *Five Fine Printers: Jack Stauffacher, Adrian Wilson, Richard Bigus, Andrew Hoyem, William Everson*. The catalog of the exhibition[10] edited by Sandra Kirshenbaum, opens with the following *incipit* that pays homage to our roots as a civilization of the book:

We have our best existence within the element of Language. And the book is a concentration of that element, a whole realization of our experience in the world of ideas, and as such, it is a thing of infinite possibility....
　　　　　　　　　　　　　　　　　　　—N. Scott Momaday

In her introduction Kirshenbaum carefully identifies three streams of book art. The first is "a new genre called 'Artists' Books'" characterized as "a superb means of personal communication and aesthetic expression by contemporary artists — painters, sculptors, printmakers – who have flocked to the book as never before.... These books are art objects, aesthetic canvases; they are erratic, exotic, experimental, anti-traditional: they are sometimes careless and shoddy in workmanship, and may be deliberately ignorant of basic typographic principles, but frequently they are exciting and original."

The second stream is the "classic tradition of the *livre d'artiste* or *livre de peintre*, brought to perfection by the artists of the School of Paris (Picasso, Matisse, Bonnard, Léger, Dufy) in the early- to mid-twentieth century. These books, usually luxurious, printed on handmade paper and illustrated with original graphics, are intended as a vehicle for an artist, often one who has established a reputation as a 'fine artist' rather than a 'book illustrator' .... Some of these books are 'you-look-great-on-the-wall-let's-see-how-you-look-in-a-book' productions – essentially beautiful print portfolios with a *soupçon* of text to stitch things together. The finest examples represent a high order of visual interpretation and integration with a text, a synergistic collaboration between artist and author - for example the influential Jasper Johns collaboration with Samuel Beckett, *Foirades/Fizzles* (St Petersburg Press, 1976)."

The third stream is "Printer's Books", which Kirshenbaum identifies "...for their creative impetus [which] originates and flows not from the artist/illustrator, nor from the author/publisher, but from the printer, the person who actually makes the book." Continuing this thought she stakes the claim that printer's books potentially represent the highest genre for they permit the highest degree of artistic independence. She goes on to say that they "might also be termed Typographic Books, for they draw, not just on the heritage of the visual arts, but on the entire heritage of the book as the principal conveyor of civilization via letterforms, those signs and symbols refined and distilled over centuries to conform so perfectly to the cognitive faculties of humankind."

Kirshenbaum's categories are not mutually exclusive and in rare cases all three are present in the same book – but here I am reminded of the old caution – "you can make a book *cheap* and *fast* and *good* but choose two because you can never have all three at once."

Four out of five printers depicted in the *Five Fine Printers* exhibition of 1979 are generally considered among the most influential forerunners of the current generation of literary printers in California while the fifth – and youngest – skipped town. Four of the printers presented in this current exhibition at Stanford worked directly with one or another of these masters – Felicia Rice studied with both William Everson and Jack Stauffacher in Santa Cruz, Peggy Gotthold and Larry van Velzer worked for Andrew Hoyem, and I served an apprenticeship in book design with Adrian Wilson. Of course the story does not end here or there, and multiple influences from throughout the bibliosphere are at work on us all. Carolee Campbell studied with Harry Reese at UC Santa Barbara and is influenced, typographically speaking, by elders Ward Ritchie and Saul and Lillian Marks, while the Reeses, influenced by the Something Else Press, claim no one tradition over another. The skein is loosely wrapped with traditional and non-traditional books and presses but this *is* California[11] and we *are* working out our separate visions in the shadows or under the lights of shared traditions.

Printers are notorious for their independence and books do not behave well lying open under glass. Kirshenbaum aptly opened her introduction with the observation that: "The significant items shown consist largely of books, and books do not like exhibits, do not like to be "pinned" like butterflies under glass or on walls. Their beauty rests not in one lovely pattern of exotic coloration but in the physical experience of their heft and texture, the firmness and elegance of the binding, the slow sequential apperception as one turns the leaves, of the white spaces ... a "fine" book in its totality is an immensely complex physical and artistic object – easy to look at, but difficult to *see*. It can be experienced fully only through the act of reading."

Kirshenbaum's third stream, the "Printer's Book," is a good place to start to describe our own collective presence. All five presses here represented print their own books at their own discretion and with little outside constraint. All have moved beyond the boundaries of commercial fine press and the comfortable fireside Arts and Crafts styles that defined fine printing as a gentleman's library preserve. They all publish experimental and contemporary literature and art in collaboration with artists and writers, often incorporating their own texts and art (e.g. Carolee Campbell's photographs, Harry Reese's paintings and poems, Larry van Velzer's texts, etc.). Each press is additionally (and significantly) distinguished by a heightened awareness of historical printing traditions, sophisticated design, masterful presswork, and attention paid to the bookbinder's art.

In the most successful works here exhibited, a heightened sensory *frisson* is imparted to the reader, magnifying the textual/visual content. This synesthesia is achieved by the artist/printer/binder incorporating unusual yet surprisingly appropriate materials intended to create a book that both resonates with, and magnifies, the impact of the text under the most intimate of conditions – in the hands, ears, and even more subtly, in the nostrils of the reader.

I speak here of the sound of a cascading river as one opens the Ninja Press edition of *The Real World of Manuel Córdova*, the ultralight rustling of leaves in the Foolscap Press edition of *Direction of the Road*, the thrill of handling an ancient Mayan manuscript in the *Codex Espangliensis* from Moving Parts Press, and the dangerous presence of a rat-trap concealed inside a gold ingot in *The Standard* from the Turkey Press.

Each of the presses in this exhibition has created its own identity and sustains a complex of collaborations that defy categorization. Yet it is most certainly in the masterful complexity of these books that we find beauty and inspiration in valiant combat with a benumbed world oversaturated with information while at the same time drained of meaning.

NOTES

For the works appearing in the notes below, full citations are given in the Further Reading section at the end of the book.

1 Everson 1992: xi.

2 Everson 1974.

3 "When I am in California, I am not in the West. I am west of the West." —Theodore Roosevelt.

4 Butor 1968: 39.

5 Everson 1992: 91.

6 Hart 1985. Ward Ritchie 1987. Kirshenbaum and Karmiole 1987.

7 Lauf and Phillpot 1998.

8 Drucker 1995.

9 Koch 2010a.

10 Kirshenbaum 1979.

11 A sign of the continuing vitality of the book arts in California is the emergence in 2007 of the Berkeley-based CODEX International Book Fair and Symposium. The 2009 Book Fair, recently hailed as the most successful in the world, included over 150 exhibiting artists and printers gathered from six continents and representing over 20 countries.

The CODEX Foundation, beginning in 2011, will collaborate with Stanford University Press to publish books and monographs dedicated to documenting the arts of the book on the global scale. The foundation's first major publication: *Book Art Object* (David Jury and Peter Koch eds. The CODEX Foundation. Berkeley. 2008. 478 pp. heavily illustrated in full color) supersedes all previous efforts at documenting the contemporary book arts scene. The foundation immediately followed up by initiating a series of monographs (now up to number six) by prominent international typographers, book artists, and printers (in the following order):

Why There Are Pages and Why They Must Turn. Robert Bringhurst. CODE(X)+1 Series number 1. CODEX, Berkeley. 2008.

Art Definition Five and Other Writings. Peter Rutledge Koch. CODE(X)+1 Series number 2. CODEX, Berkeley. 2008.

Each New Book. Alan Loney. CODE(X)+1 Series number 3. CODEX, Berkeley 2008.

<Usus>, Typography, and Artists' Books. Ulrike Stoltz & Ute Schneider. CODE(X)+1 Series number 4. CODEX, Berkeley. 2010.

Visionaries and Fanatics: Type Design and the Private Press. Russell Maret. CODE(X)+1 Series number 5. CODEX, Berkeley. 2010.

L'acide brut manifesto. Didier Mutel. CODE(X)+1 Series number 6. CODEX, Berkeley. 2011.

All of the presses in this exhibition have exhibited at all of the CODEX book fairs to date (2007, 2009, and 2011), and all appeared in the first volume of *Book Art Object*.

CURATOR'S NOTE

The Art of the Book in California: Five Contemporary Presses is the result of a collaboration between the presses themselves, the writers, and the hosts of the exhibition. The texts introducing the presses and describing their books are in the words of their makers. This was the result of a deliberate decision to allow the individual voice of each press to continue unbroken from the books in the exhibition out into the catalogue.

Foolscap Press

For us, each new book is like a first trip to Paris (or London or Florence) - we don't know exactly what the experience will hold but we're excited. We think we know what we want to see and do, but that can all change depending on our surroundings, on the materials at hand. We will do what's practicable. Let us not hurry our stay but take the time to explore all the possibilities while we're here - a missed opportunity is not part of our plan. So, each new book is an unfamiliar environment. When we have finished and finally leave it, it is not that "we'll always have Paris," but that we'll have a book we can always return to with a sense of satisfaction.

As talk is the cheapest commodity we have, we do a lot of it between ourselves. As partners we have learned to collaborate in every sense of the word. Our biggest challenge is to discover how best to spend our creative hours. For better or worse, there are no boundaries between our private and our working lives. Because one cannot set aside a special time to discover a great idea, our project-seeking selves always accompany us, like small children, whether we are visiting a great museum or simply grocery shopping. We'd be lost without them.

Sometimes, as we begin to pursue an idea, we don't know whether we are developing a project for a printed book, a piece of ephemera, a staged marionette play, or a filmed shadow-puppet play because we don't often see a distinction between work and play. Because the process of exploration is basically the same, at some point we must ask ourselves, "Where is this going?" We might be merely entertaining each other while folding paper in the bindery or at the dinner table passing around ideas. Just as an initially blank piece of paper gets notations, an idea develops, acquires history and dialogue, and then becomes something greater.

If the idea becomes a book, we always think in multiples. There are things you can do for a one-of-a-kind book that you cannot do in an edition of 100 or 200 books, so we must make adjustments as we plan and develop a project.

In all stages of book design there are many decisions to be made and therefore many opportunities to add fresh ideas to the project. Any initial idea may get molded and reshaped in the process while the thinking is still fluid. Sometimes these changes in plans are due to physical limitations of the materials and sometimes to creative inspiration – and sometimes the first can happily bring about the second.

We have a philosophy that leaves us free to stumble into anything that works in regard to process, design and materials. And that philosophy is that we try not to believe that we are the masters of anything. Having said that, we do find that we are traditionalists in this sense: we want our books, above all, to be well made, to be a good read and, when we are done, we want them to handle like books.

We draw inspiration from something written by the Russian puppeteer Sergei Obraztsov. He was also an actor and spoke of Constantin Stanislavski, the great theatre theorist, and said that the man possessed "youthfulness in the perception of life, a keen sense of the truth, the will to struggle uncompromisingly for it. . . ." Obraztsov once recalled finding Stanislavski surrounded by actors young enough to be his children. They were there to learn from the Master, of course, but it was Stanislavski who seemed the youngest, the one who most of all wanted to learn something new about theatre.

We aspire always to be curious, to discover, everyday if possible, something new or interesting or different – or just puzzlingly funny. We want to discover something new about art and about fine bookmaking.

Collectively, our books do not have a unifying look to them. Each exists because there was some spark that intrigued us, the knowledge that we had never been there before. Our wish is for you the viewer and reader when seeing our books to discover something you weren't expecting, something that surprises and delights you. When this happens we are pleased, for then we know that you have shared in our revelation – you also have found something new.

1.
Herakles and the Eurystheusian Twelve-Step Program
Lawrence G. Van Velzer. Illustrations by Peggy Gotthold. 2009.

Fifty-two panels, Curtis Holcomb and Hahnemüle Bugra paper, Tiepelo type. Japanese cloth over boards, Printed label and printed paper sleeve.

Edition of 100 copies, plus 10 copies *hors commerce*. 11.25 x 6.75 inches. (When opened, the width varies from 12.50 to 33.00 inches.)

Following the long tradition of reimagining and adapting the Greek legends, this is a retelling of the Twelve Labors of Herakles. *Here, the story is told completely in dialogue between Herakles and his half-brother King Eurystheus. Herakles certainly has an anger management problem. What better way to frame the myth of his twelve labors than to frame Herakles' experience as a contemporary twelve-step program so prevalent in today's society?*

The story is told in panels, each ending in an illustration of a vase on which a labor is described in a line drawing. Each labor is visible as a separate episode. The book can be viewed, read, and displayed in many configurations. The book, sewn in accordion form, can be stood on end and the pages fanned out in several directions. It also can be read conventionally in double-page spreads. A printed wrapper slides over the outside of the book, to contain and protect it.

Because the stories of the Greek myths are so often told on vases, we thought we could tell the story on vases in a contemporary yet timeless way with shadow puppets in a movie. The text and story of the movie follow the dialogue in the book, with the different labors acted by shadow puppets, as Herakles and King Eurystheus discuss what you are seeing. Rather than just showing the movie, we wanted to make a fitting movie palace, or in this case a movie temple, in which the movie could be seen. The classical proscenium is made of painted paper.

2.
Despatches
Michael Katakis. Photographs by Michael Katakis. 2008.

Three separate books each 24 pages in length, housed in a dispatch case, Magnani Vergata paper for the text, Hahnemüle Ingres for the covers, and O'Malley crackle Cave Paper for the dispatch case, Garamond type. The photographs: archival pigment prints, printed by Deborah Mills Thackrey of Willow Glen Productions, using Epson Ultrachrome inks on 100 percent cotton, acid-free, Velvet Fine Art paper.

Edition of 185 copies. 8.40 x 4.60 inches.

Originally written as journal entries, Despatches is a selection from Michael Katakis' records of many years' travel and reflections. These writings bring the immediacy of an eyewitness report even as they convey a perceptive image of Michael Katakis' own past. The deliberate spelling of 'Despatches' pays homage to T.E. Lawrence, Gertrude Bell and Mungo Park, who, as Michael says, "helped a solitary little boy dream of deserts and faraway places." These are not travel guides but are more personal, as if we were reading letters from the most desirable sort of friend - a friend who, though far away, carries you with him as he meanders through the medina in Fez, or strides along in the tall elephant grass of Sierra Leone. The center spread of each book has a map of the region showing the locations associated with those journal entries.

Each of the three booklets focuses on a different country: Sierra Leone, Morocco, and Greece. The books fit into a case formed of handmade paper from Cave Paper, made to look like a timeworn dispatch case.

3.
Direction of the Road
Ursula Le Guin. Anamorphic woodcut by Aaron Johnson. 2007.

Linen wrapper, text and cover paper from St. Armand, Bembo type. Box covered in Japanese cloth.

Edition: 120 numbered copies, plus 30 copies *hors commerce*. 40 pages. 14.40 x 10.50 inches.

Ursula Le Guin's short story is told from the perspective of an oak tree. At first, the nearby dirt road next to the tree sees only the occasional passerby and the tree has no trouble with the process of looming up to meet the traveler, and then diminishing as the traveler recedes into the distance. But as the roadway traffic increases, and the pace increases, with horse-drawn buggies and then cars on the paved highway, the oak has to master an increasingly complex series of maneuvers, both growing in one direction and shrinking in the opposite.

We approached artist Aaron Johnson, whose paintings and woodcuts of trees we have long admired, to create a very special tree for this project. This tree needed to show movement and we decided that the ancient technique of anamorphic art was an ideal response to Le Guin's short story narrated by a tree. The anamorphic woodcut, a portrait of an oak, mirrors the trick of perception described by Le Guin.

The art is presented as part of the custom-made box that also houses the cylindrical mirror and the book. The book is sewn into a handmade paper cover made by St. Armand Mill. The text paper, also by St. Armand, is a linen wrapper, which sounds like the rustling of leaves as you turn the pages.

4.
Other Worlds: A Journey to the Moon
Cyrano de Bergerac. Translation and Introduction by Geoffrey Strachan. Eight direct gravure etchings by Leslie Lerner. 2004.

Hahnemüle Bugra paper, Garamond type. Bound in goatskin and Japanese cloth, housed in a Japanese cloth-covered box.

Edition: 120 copies, plus 8 printer's proofs numbered i-viii. 120 pages. 11.56 x 9.40 inches.

The book opens to an image of the moon, engraved by Claude Mellan (1598–1688) in 1636. He viewed the moon through one of Galileo's telescopes. Around this image are satellites drawn by Leslie Lerner and also used later in the book for the chapter openings. Using the twentieth-century unbowdlerized version of the text as a basis for his (revised) translation, Geoffrey Strachan wrote a comprehensive introduction, placing Cyrano de Bergerac clearly in his seventeenth-century context, at a time when the telescope was newly invented. De Bergerac, whom most people confuse with the caricature from Edmond Rostand's nineteenth-century play, was an accomplished writer in at least three standard genres of his time. As Geoffrey Strachan notes, "His letters show elegance, wit, pungent rhetoric, and a feeling for nature. His comedy shows Rabelaisian verve, with its larger-than-life characters and satire on pedantry. His tragedy, on the other hand, shows considerable formal discipline and Cornelian eloquence. But it was only in L'Autre Monde (Other Worlds) that Cyrano found a genre that gave full scope to his gifts, the diversity of his interests and the modernity of his spirit." In his informative introduction Geoffrey Strachan also speaks of "pataphysics," a term used by Alfred Jarry to denote the science of imaginary solutions, and states, "If ever there was a classic example of pataphysics in action it is surely Cyrano's decision to resolve his contemporaries' disputes about the nature of the moon by penning an imaginary flight there — in order, as it were, to see for himself: a perfect marriage between empirical method and poetic imagination."

The eight etchings by Leslie Lerner show a world at once familiar and unknowable. Much in the prints echoes the atmosphere of the artist's paintings and show another world whose landscape is replete with many of the symbols familiar to those acquainted with "The Man With The Wooden Arm," the artist's alter ego, a seventeenth-century traveler from Delft. Lerner felt that the images "would interact with the narrative images, creating a hybrid space. That hybrid space would serve as a parallel dislocation matching the quirkiness of the de Bergerac text."

5.
The Tower of the Winds
Lawrence G. Van Velzer and Peggy Gotthold. 2002.

Historical illustrations, unpaginated scroll, 25 feet long, Zerkall Book paper, Adobe Herculanum type. Payrus endsheet; scroll housed in a formed and dyed paper case.

Edition of 200 copies. 10.75 inches x 25 feet, case 11.00 x 2.75 inches diameter.

The text of the Tower of the Winds follows the written history and compiled science of an intriguing building, constructed in the first century B.C. as a monument to mythology and to house the most advanced scientific instruments of the day. The Tower has had many functions both mechanical and spiritual, and much has been "explained" by scholars from Antiquity up to the present time. Early observers include Marcus Vitruvius, the Roman architect, and Varro; both left descriptions of the building. A Turkish traveler in the seventeenth century speculated on the magical properties of the construction. In the mid-1700s, British architects James Stuart and Nicolas Revett published several volumes of the Antiquities of Athens, one of which contains detailed descriptions and exquisite drawings of the Tower of the Winds, with meticulous notes of the measurements of the building. In the twentieth century, Derek De Sola-Price took up the task of explaining the uses of the Tower, and came away with a theory that the Greeks, in addition to a water clock, had a sophisticated geared apparatus capable of showing the time and the positions of the planets and stars. Each of these records exposes the biases of the various observers, from the meticulous precision of the engravings of Stuart and Revett, to the Turkish traveler's fascination with magic, to the accumulation of scientific proof by De Sola-Price. Fittingly, in its scroll form, the act of reading this book becomes a meditation on the concept of time.

For the scroll case we dyed 640-gram watercolor paper and shaped it into a cylinder. Inside the case, we placed a map of Ancient Athens, which shows the position of the tower in relation to the Acropolis. The Tower of the Winds can still be seen today in the Roman Agora at Athens. It is

a glorious survivor in a field of ruined columns and it is a monument for which, according to one modern scholar, "there is nothing comparable in all of Greek architecture..."

6.
Desert Dreams
Lawrence G. Van Velzer. Illustrated by Peggy Gotthold. 1997.

Legion Letterpress paper, Stymie type. Multiple colored illustrations hand inked using stencils and added watercolor. Bound in Japanese cloth and Bugra label over boards.
Edition: 185 copies. 144 pages. 8.06 x 9.31 inches.

This is a tale from the heart of the Great Middle Desert where three of its rather unusual denizens inhabit an arid and enchanting land. The first is Tommy, a young tumbleweed with a longing to travel to the distant horizon and learn about the mountains that so intrigue him. The second character is Dusty, a dust devil whose array of hats are fashioned from fine sand and who considers herself the desert's foremost detective. Then there is Crawfoot, a crow caught between his desire to remain within his accustomed surroundings and the unexpected opportunity to add to his formidable collection of shiny things. The three companions set out on a journey far from their familiar environment in exploration and discovery.

The story was inspired by the many trips Larry's family took to the deserts of Southern California. Here, the desert was always a place of magic for the children - an exotic environment for the full potential of magic, where a dust devil seemed to have a life of its own and one could be chased by tumbleweed in an afternoon breeze.

After creating the art for the book, we decided to brayer multiple colors directly onto the printing plates and print those colors in a single pass through the press. We used this method throughout the book. Afterward, we applied additional watercolor to some of the illustrations.

Moving Parts Press

Felicia Rice is a native Californian rarely found far from the coast. Born in San Francisco, she was raised in the Bay Area art scene of the 1950s and 1960s. The founding faculty of the Mendocino Art Center, her parents became her first and most important teachers. At nineteen Felicia discovered her future vocation: the art of the book.

In 1974 she moved to Santa Cruz to attend the University of California there and study typography and letterpress printing under designer-printer Jack Stauffacher at Cowell College. During that time, she had the opportunity to work with William Everson, poet-printer in the Lime Kiln Press at the McHenry Library on his renowned book, *Granite and Cypress. She also worked* with Sherwood Grover, pressman for thirty years at the long-lived and preeminent Grabhorn Press in San Francisco, and in 1981 she inherited Sherwood's press and type library. Other influences include noted printmakers Nick De Matties, Kay Metz, and Garner Tullis.

In 1977 Felicia founded Moving Parts Press in Santa Cruz where she entertained clients and authors, artists and students for over a decade before moving the press to the mountains of Bonny Doon. The Moving Parts Press logo depicts a multi-armed freak from an edition of the *Nuremberg Chronicle* pirated and printed in Augsburg in 1497, and it also evokes Kali, the Hindu goddess associated with eternal energy. Under the Moving Parts Press imprint, and occasionally the subsidiary Mutant Drone Press, Felicia has created and published hundreds of books, broadsides, prints, and ephemera. These editions of new literature, works in translation, and contemporary art explore the relationship of word and image, typography and the visual arts, the fine arts and popular culture, political criticism and social impact. Felicia employs traditional typography and bookmaking methods together with digital technology, bringing the flexibility of screen-based design to the texture and historical tradition of the letterpress-printed page. Each piece is a performance of the text and the text is the source material informing an indescribable whole.

The Literatura Chicana/Latina Series and Livres d'Artiste Series are two areas of inquiry that have both challenged and sustained the editorial and artistic direction of the press. The Literatura Chicana/Latina Series of contemporary Chicano/Latino artists and writers in translation explores the intersection of cultures, disciplines and book structures in both limited and trade editions. Each book is the result of a close collaboration with visual artists, performing and sound artists, and writers, resulting in book structures in which word and image meet and merge. Most notable among these works is the *Codex Espangliensis*, a book that chronicles and confronts the realities and surrealities of border culture. Having garnered international attention, the trade edition has remained in print continuously since 1998. Felicia's current project, *Documentado/Undocumented*, builds on this success with the addition of her own imagery, a video, and an electronic soundscape.

A prime example of the Livres d'Artiste Series is *Cosmogonie intime/An Intimate Cosmogony*, published in 2005. Here, five long poems presented in the original French and in English are at once intimate and universal, and offer insight into a poetic journey that illuminates our common humanity. The French *livres d'artiste*, early-twentieth- century limited editions integrating visual and poetic text, were among the crowning achievements of the twentieth-century book, and this series of publications interprets them for present-day audiences.

Work from the Press has been included in countless exhibitions and collections both nationally and internationally, from the AIGA Annual Book Shows in New York and Frankfurt to the Victoria & Albert Museum. Moving Parts Press has been the recipient of numerous awards and grants including a Rydell Fellowship Award, a Stiftung Buchkunst Schönste Bücher aus aller Welt Ehrendiplom, and grants from the NEA, CAC, and the French Ministry of Culture. A catalogue of the high points of Felicia's work can be found at her website, www.movingpartspress.com.

Felicia Rice designed and printed work on commission for over twenty years and taught book arts at the University of California, Santa Cruz (UCSC), for fourteen years before becoming director of the Extension graphic design program there. She currently manages UCSC's Digital Arts and New Media MFA Program, satisfying a lifelong interest in art education.

1.

Documentado/Undocumented Ars Shamánica Performática

Performance texts by Guillermo Gómez-Peña. Videography by Gustavo Vazquez. Critical commentary by Jennifer González. Sound art by Zachary Watkins. Work-in-progress.

Documentado/Undocumented is a long-term collaboration between the book artist/performance artist/writer Guillermo Gómez-Peña and filmmaker Gustavo Vazquez, as well as sound artist/engineer Zachary Watkins and art historian and critic Jennifer González. A 2009 Rydell Award made it possible to realize ideas in development since 2007 as a prototype. The next phase of the project, *The Myth of Fingerprints*, was completed in 2010.

The accordian-fold book features Gómez-Peña's performance texts and Rice's relief prints and expressive typography, accompanied by critical commentary by González. It is housed in a hi-tech aluminum trunk containing a DVD, an altar, and a cabinet of curiosities such as custom-made Mexican wrestling masks and ritual objects. Opening the box and handling the objects within will trigger Watkins' sound art.

Book: Edition of 50 copies. 17.75 x 11.13 inches.
Box: Edition of 15. 16.75 x 19.00 x 4.00 inches, with individual compartments holding ritual objects

Guillermo Gómez-Peña has been exploring intercultural issues with the use of mixed genres and experimental language since the 1970s. A MacArthur Fellow, he is a regular contributor to the national radio news magazine "All Things Considered" (National Public Radio), a writer for newspapers and magazines in the U.S. and Mexico, and a contributing editor to "The Drama Review" (MIT). We worked together in the 1990s on the Codex Espangliensis with great success.

My earliest notes for this collaboration date from a 2007 meeting with Gómez-Peña. In this meeting we sketched out a project comprising a book and video: the book would be developed in response to a video that he and filmmaker Gustavo Vazquez had been working on for some time. Over the next few years our brainstorming sessions grew to include two new collaborators. The book project evolved into one part of an exciting and complex installation piece that bridges the book and the art worlds. With the help of Jennifer González, my research took me into the history of collecting, of the museum and the freak shows of the nineteenth century, and into unusual materials and new methods. This work-in-progress has caused me to redefine myself as a book artist who works not only with the book as the bearer of text and image, but the book as performance art, a stage for the performance of text and image.

2.

El alfabeto animado / The Lively Alphabet / Uywakunawan Qelqasqa

Text by Monica Brown. Translation into Quechua by Jenny Callañaupa Huarhua. 2009.

This trilingual alphabet book in Spanish, English, and Quechua, a Native American language of South America, grew out of a dream, a chance meeting, and dedicated working friendships. The text is the work of renowned children's book author, Monica Brown, translated into Quechua by Jenny Callañaupa Huarhua, and interpreted in a series of drawings by Felicia Rice. The book is populated by hand-knit finger puppets imported from Peru, set in scenes drawn and printed at Moving Parts Press on a rainbow of cloth from Cusco, Peru.

El alfabeto animado is letterpress-printed in black from zinc photoengravings on woolen cloth known as *bayeta*. The binding is the result of the work of Peter Burnes, Maureen Carey, and Susan Else. The book is housed in a cloth-covered box made by Maureen Carey.

Edition of 8 copies. 15 pages. 19.75 x 25.50 inches

Some years ago I had a dream of a pillow-sized fabric book populated by finger puppets from Latin America set in scenes printed in black. When children's book designer Katie Jennings contacted me about her deep appreciation of my earlier collaborative work with Enrique Chagoya and Guillermo Gómez-Peña, Codex Espangliensis, I invited her for a visit. It was during this exchange about books, typography, and technology, letterpress printing, poetry and politics that I introduced Katie to my dream book. I had already begun collecting finger puppets through friends and family traveling in the Andes. Katie encouraged me to bring this book to life.

Katie talked about her experiences as a children's book designer and the world of children's book publication. As a maker of limited edition artists' books I make an effort to bring my creations to a larger audience as trade editions widely available through booksellers everywhere. Katie suggested that Peruvian-American author Monica Brown might be interested in collaborating on a very limited edition of artists' books that would be translated into a trade edition.

El alfabeto animado is the result of our efforts to bring this to pass. In the words of translator, Jenny Callañaupa Huarhua, "Thank you very much for giving me the opportunity to become a part of this wonderful work; for me it is an honor to contribute to this as it demonstrates once again that when you have the desire to do something, your friends and colleagues will respond to your call and what might have been an overwhelming undertaking yields gratifying results."

3.
Cosmogonie Intime / An Intimate Cosmogony
Poems by Yves Peyré. Translation by Elizabeth R. Jackson. Drawings by Ray Rice. 2005.

An Intimate Cosmogony presents five long poems in French and English by contemporary French poet Yves Peyré, with an English translation by Elizabeth R. Jackson. The five poems are a sequence that carries the poet himself and his generation through time and space, touching base regularly to evoke a familiar name, a place, a far gone era. Pen-and-ink drawings by Ray Rice are enriched with multiple colors using the *pochoir* or stenciling process. The deluxe edition is hand-painted in watercolor throughout by the artist.

The type is composed digitally using Janson types and letterpress printed from zinc photoengravings on Fabriano Artistico paper. The binding by Craig Jenson of BookLab II, of San Marcos, Texas, responds to the model of the early-twentieth-century French *livre d'artiste*; the accordion-fold book block rests in a printed paper cover wrapped in glassine. It is housed in a paper slipcase and a cloth-covered box.

Edition of 72 and 12 hand-painted deluxe copies. 15.00 x 10.00 inches

Yves Peyré is, and has been, very engaged in artists' books through his recent role as Director of the Bibliothèque littéraire Jacques Doucet, the French government's library of first editions, manuscripts and publications of modern French literature. He is a member of the circle of writers and artists whose work makes up the Doucet collection, and has also written extensively on the twentieth-century livre d'artiste.

I felt it was important for Cosmogonie intime to build on the traditions of the livre d'artiste. I employed hand-colored images using a traditional French stenciling process known as pochoir, and designed a very simple portfolio-style binding. I was excited to add to the Moving Parts Press Livres d'Artiste Series that began in 1993 with Meidosems, my first project with translator Elizabeth R. Jackson, old family friend and professor of French literature.

On a very personal note, the artist for this project was my father, Ray Rice, who died in 2001 at the age of eighty-five within a year of completing his part of Cosmogonie Intime. His rich career as an artist was driven by a strong Midwestern work ethic and unswerving internal compass.

He spent more than sixty years on the American art scene and his list of *awards, exhibitions and commissions extends back to the early 1950s. This book was our fourth collaboration.*

4.
Codex Espangliensis: From Columbus to the Border Patrol
Performance texts by Guillermo Gómez-Peña. Collage imagery by Enrique Chagoya. 1998.

The work chronicles and confronts the realities and surrealities of border culture. Collage images by Enrique Chagoya juxtapose examples of graphic art from pre-Hispanic times to present-day Mexico with traditions of Western art and contemporary American pop culture. The series of performance texts and poems were selected from Guillermo Gómez-Peña's works over his twenty-year career. The marriage of the two is the work of Felicia Rice.

Codex Espangliensis is letterpress-printed in black and red from zinc photoengravings on Amatl paper lined with Shintengujo tissue. The texts appear in a variety of typefaces designed to evoke the excitement of the Gómez-Peña's stage performance. The book is housed in an Amatl paper and Canapetta black book cloth Shiho chitsu-style portfolio box made by Maureen Carey. Signed by the author, artist and printer.

Edition of 40 and 5 hand-painted deluxe copies. 15 spreads. 9.00 x 11.38 inches (extends to 31.00 feet)

My parents met as art students in New York City in the 1930s when the art world was permeated with the politics of the Depression, the Labor Movement and Left vs. Right. Family mythology includes the 1949 trip from Vermont to Mexico to apprentice with the muralist Siqueiros, only to have my sisters, one and four years old, become so ill that the family barely escaped to the north intact; all this before I was born. Throughout my life, my parents' circle included former apprentices of Diego Rivera, and friends of Frida Kahlo. As a young child I would sneak into my father's studio to study Posada's prints sensationalizing fire, murder, freakish

births. I grew up in California with the legacy of the Spanish land grants, the Californios, the Mexican muralists and their saints (San Francisco, Santa Cruz). I am a member of a hybrid community of immigrants and artists; we use multiple languages.

It took five years to complete the Codex Espangliensis. Through time it slowly grew to dominate my efforts at Moving Parts Press: the Press, which had been a public place with clients and students coming and going daily, became a private studio devoted to the development of a monumental work. The Codex shifted the emphasis of my book work from the literary to the sculptural, drawing upon models of the Mesoamerican codex, western European bookmaking and Japanese binding structures.

5.
A Canticle to the Waterbirds
William Everson. Woodcuts by Daniel O. Stolpe. Alcatraz Editions. 1992.

A Canticle to the Waterbirds is, by his own account, William Everson's best-known poem. Here it is accompanied by woodcuts by Daniel O. Stolpe, and designed and printed by Felicia Rice in collaboration with Gary Young under the Alcatraz Editions imprint in tribute to Everson in his last years. Former apprentices Peter Thomas and Maureen Carey also contributed to the execution of this work. In addition to the poem, there is both an author's note by Everson and a printer's note.

A Canticle to the Waterbirds is letterpress-printed on Thomas's handmade paper in black with three gray and one polychrome woodcut. The poem was handset in Weiss types. The books are casebound by Carey in linen book cloth with a printed label framed by red Moriki paper.

Edition of 61 copies. 24 pages. 13.00 x 19.00 inches

"A Canticle to the Waterbirds" was written for the Feast of Saint Francis of Assisi in 1950, early in William Everson's Catholic life. In 1982 a group of printers, former apprentices and others active in the book arts in

the Santa Cruz area formed a loose organization, the Printers' Chappel of Santa Cruz. William Everson closed his introduction to the catalog for our 1986 exhibition with this passage, "In my old age I called on the spirit of Jeffers, my early master, and inducted a generation of student printers into the ordeal of hewing out a masterpiece from the recalcitrance of type, paper and ink. Now they are doubling back, founding their own presses, and following writers unconsciously spelling out the ethos of this region in the ineluctable articulation of the Word." Five of these former apprentices and friends came together to create this book in tribute to Everson, a master of the hand press and one of the finest poet-printers of the 20th century. The press name was not associated with any of the participants, but chosen specifically for this use. In the author's note, Everson wrote, "I take joy in the company of my apprentices who learned well everything I taught them, without requirement. The consolations of life yield such evocative dimensions."

6.

Weygandt/Prints
Prints by Donald Weygandt. Poems by Tim Fitzmaurice, Madeline Moore, Eliane C. Roe, and David Swanger. 1991.

Weygandt/Prints is a series of six prints by Donald Weygandt which are presented in a portfolio box and accompanied by a limited edition chapbook. This work takes timeless everyday vessels such as pots, pitchers and vases as its subject.

The prints are reproduced using lithographic, intaglio and linoleum- cut techniques. Each is printed on Rives BFK Cream paper and signed and numbered by the artist. The portfolio box, covered with black Japanese book cloth shot with gold, is lined with a patterned paper designed by the artist. The boxes were made by Maureen Carey with Sabrina Hall, Felicia Rice and Elizabeth Wallen.

A chapbook, including three original prints and a statement from the artist, rests in a pocket inside the front cover of the portfolio. David Swanger, Tim Fitzmaurice, Eliane Corbeil Roe and Madeline Moore contributed poems inspired by Weygandt's prints.

The chapbook was handset in Garamond types and letterpress printed on Mohawk Superfine, Moriki and Rives papers.

Print portfolio: Edition of 20 signed and numbered copies with 10 artist's proofs, 2 archival proofs, 2 studio proofs and 12 printer's proofs. 14 pages. 18.00 x 18.00 inches. Chapbook: Edition of 400. 9.00 x 6.00 inches

Don Weygandt has achieved regional renown as both a painter and a printmaker. He was a member of the arts faculty at the University of California, Santa Cruz, from 1967–1991. Colleague Douglas McClellan writes, "His touch is the touch of an angel but there is a mischief in it: a turn of a line, a slab of color, a push at an edge, an elusive asymmetry, any of these might connive the form to a surprising sense of delight…. Each work has total authority and not a little magic."

For fourteen years I was a part-time instructor at UCSC. Class meetings were held in my studio and focused on printing and publishing limited editions that incorporated text and image by UCSC art and writing faculty. These publications remain as a snapshot of creative life on campus at the time. This print portfolio was produced with a cadre of students and staff in honor of Don's retirement after twenty-four years as founding faculty of the art department of a new university.

So often artists are asked to respond to texts, most often as "illustrators"; in this case I wanted to reverse the roles of artist and writer. The day the Gulf War erupted in 1991, I had invited writers from across campus to Moving Parts Press to view Don's prints and take away impressions for their contributions to the chapbook. Only four followed through, as the war seemed to overwhelm many others' desire to write. Madeline Moore's poem speaks directly to the war.

Ninja Press

Ninja Press was founded in 1984 by Carolee Campbell who is its sole proprietor. While there was no specific literary agenda governing the selection of works to be published by the press at the outset, the abiding interest has been, in the main, contemporary poetry. Carolee's decision to embark on the path of bookmaking came from her extensive experience as a photographer, her darkroom work with both nineteenth- and twentieth-century photographic processes, and her gallery showings. Turning photographic sequences into bound books ushered her into bookbinding, followed by working on experimental book structures. Eventually, she expanded her work into letterpress printing, thereby opening the way into contemporary poetry – confronting it for the first time with a directness and depth of understanding she had seldom experienced as a reader.

Carolee's artistic training began in the theatre in Los Angeles, when she was age fifteen. Within five years, she had made her way to New York City to continue training as an actor with Uta Hagen. She traveled and worked in theatres in many parts of the country, but she always returned to New York, following her passion of early years. It was her theatre training — her work in many plays, including those of Chekhov, Shakespeare, Tennessee Williams, and Arthur Miller - that laid the groundwork for her love of research, discipline, and process that she now sustains in her bookwork. Further, her training with Lee Strasberg in the Stanislavski system or method taught her a controlled balance between the rational – process and technique – and the irrational – intuition; this is evident in the design and realization of each new book.

In 1976 she left a distinguished acting career, traveled in Japan, and eight years later she started Ninja Press (named in honor of Ninja, her first and best black cat) and in 2004 she celebrated its twentieth anniversary with a retrospective exhibition, *Ninja Press at Twenty*. After opening at UCLA's Williams Andrews Clark Memorial Library, for the next two years it went on to the University of Arizona; UC San Diego; the University of Texas, San Antonio; and UC Santa Barbara. In November 2010, a retrospective exhibition, *Ninja Press: Twenty-Five Years & Counting* opened at Lafayette College in Easton, Pennsylvania.

All Ninja Press books, broadsides, and keepsakes are handset in metal type and printed letterpress on a Vandercook Universal I flatbed proof press. Carolee designs, sets, prints, and binds each of the editions at the press.

From the outset, one of Ninja Press's primary mandates was to strive for the highest standards of excellence in craftsmanship and quality while attempting to find new approaches to the union between word, image, and book structure. That mission will continue to fuel the inspiration for future edition works, as well as one-of-a-kind books.

1.
The Persephones
Nathaniel Tarn. 2009.

These are ten long, multifaceted poems that orbit around the myths of Persephone, Hades, and Demeter. The book consists of twelve unbound folios, each of which has been hand painted on both front and back with sumi ink and salt; each book is unique. The poems are printed on and alongside the artwork on dampened Domestic Etching, in hand-set Van Dijck with Weiss Initials Series I for the display. The folios are held in a goat parchment cover, a hard-sided chemise wrapper of deep green Asahi Japanese silken cloth, and a slipcase covered in natural-colored linen. Design, sumi paintings, presswork, and binding are by Carolee Campbell, with binding assistance from Karen Skove Chu. The slipcases are made by Judi Conant in Guildhall, Vermont.

Edition of 85 numbered copies and 12 *hors commerce*. 48pp. 14.25 x 9.25 inches.

"Tarn belongs to a secret lineage in modern poetry: the ecstatic erudites. Along with such predecessors as MacDiarmid, Rukeyser, and Rexroth, his poetry is a conjunction of eroticism, radical politics, Eastern philosophy and Western mysticism, world myth and the world's arts, contemporary science, and precise descriptions of the natural world. The poem is the place for everything, complex thoughts are presented directly, simple things find new words, and all the stuff of the world is there to celebrate or excoriate, but above all, to investigate."

—Eliot Weinberger

The Persephones, *the second Ninja Press publication of the work of Nathaniel Tarn, was first published in 1974 by Christopher's Books in Santa Barbara, California, in a small chapbook format. Much of the edition was subsequently destroyed by fire. The poems were significantly altered by the poet in 2007 for this Ninja Press edition.*

2.
Pruned Boughs
Michael Hannon. 2008.

This book of previously unpublished poems is the third in a series of Ninja Press publications written by this generous and highly favored poet. The type is hand set in Meridian with Weiss Initials Series III for the display and printed letterpress on dampened Frankfurt in three colors. From a punch cut by Carolee Campbell, then struck into a matrix and cast by Theo Rehak, the decorative device used throughout is printed and hand-brushed with iridescent mica. The book is sewn into dark walnut-stained handmade flax paper from Cave Paper. With its rich walnut covers and stark white text, this slender volume brings into sharp relief the somber prospect invoked by these poems. Design, presswork, and binding are by Carolee Campbell, with binding assistance from Karen Skove Chu.

Edition of 100 numbered copies and 12 *hors commerce.* 24 pp. 10.00 x 3.00 inches.

"Pruned Boughs, *first symptoms of an involuntary deconstruction, previous poetic habits exploded, the words themselves laid bare, & beginning to insist on a prosody reduced to its least unit, which is two—binary poems, an idée fixe, font of clear abstractions, poetry roots embedded in the narrow remnants of an outraged lyricism, to see afresh, what is, beyond all hope or wishing, the mortal world."*

—Michael Hannon

3.
The Intimate Stranger
Breyten Breytenbach. 2006.

In this single, long prose poem, every paragraph has been given its own page or double-page spread. Each page is embellished with signs and symbols printed in multiple colors inspired by the text. The type is hand-set Samson with Libra for the display, printed letterpress on dampened flax paper hand-made especially for this edition by Bridget O'Malley at Cave Paper. A horoscope as well as signs and symbols are drawn by Carolee Campbell and printed letterpress from photopolymer plates. Additional symbols are applied by hand using pure earth pigments. The boards are covered in flax paper hand-coated at the press with a mixture of ochre pigment and fine volcanic pumice. The text is sewn into an inner cover with thin purple silk cord. An additional purple, hard-covered enclosure with an artful locking device is made by Judi Conant in Guildhall, Vermont. A separate chapbook entitled *Legend* and containing the glossary of signs and symbols used, is printed in eight colors with three additional hand-applied pigments, on dampened Nideggen and sewn with silk cord into a flax paper cover. Design, presswork, and binding are by Carolee Campbell, with binding assistance by Karen Skove Chu.

Edition of 100 numbered copies with 10 *hors commerce.* 40pp. 13.00 x 7.50 inches.

In a language rich with streamlined ornament, Breyten Breytenbach charts the geography of the land while, on a shifting plane, he conjures the landscape of the human heart.

4.
Burn Down the Zendo
Michael Hannon. 2004.

The type is hand-set Spectrum with Felix Titling for the display, printed letterpress in two colors on Japanese gashen-shi. Each page, from the opening fly to the last poem, is inhabited by an ensō or empty circle printed from magnesium plates. The ensō, an image common to Zen Buddhist art, can mean many things: everything, nothing, unity, the moon, or even a rice cake. In this text, the ensō grows in size on each subsequent page, giving the reader the impression of passing through the center of the ensō to the other side. The cover is Egyptian tow flax hand-made at Cave Paper. David Brock has hand-inscribed the kanji on each cover with sumi ink. The kanji reads 'sanzendo', and while not idiomatic Japanese, can be read to mean: the Zen meditation hall itself; sitting in meditation in the hall; and/or the periodic question-and-answer period that takes place between Zen student and teacher. The book structure is modeled after ledger books or chōmen, in common use throughout Japan, particularly during the Edo period (1603–1868). These long, slender account books were sewn in the stab binding style at one short end and kept handy by hanging it on the wall from its sewn end. The book is housed in an acrylic slipcase. Design, presswork, and binding are by Carolee Campbell, with binding assistance from Karen Skove Chu.

Edition of 110 numbered copies plus 10 *hors commerce*. 13 pp. 5.75 x 15.00 inches

This is the second Ninja Press publication of the poems of Michael Hannon. In these incisive poems the poet juggles the nature of being and not being while simultaneously traversing the shaky quicksand that defines the landscape between the conscious mind and the human heart. As Michael Hannon has written in a poem called "April," the real passes / the unreal endures.

5.
XXIV Short Love Poems
Bruce Whiteman. 2002.

The type is hand-set Eve and Paramount, printed letterpress in four colors on dampened Japanese hanga-shi. The poems are augmented by three cyanotype photographs, a nineteenth-century photographic process in which paper is sensitized by hand with a light-sensitive emulsion and contact printed using a negative. Carolee Campbell, the photographer, sensitized and printed the cyanotypes on handmade paper from the Velké Losiny mill in the Czech Republic. The boards on the accordion-style binding are covered with hand-painted paste paper by Claire Maziarczyk. Japanese iridescent cloth is on the spine. Design, presswork, and binding are by Carolee Campbell, with binding assistance from Karen Skove Chu.

Edition of 135 copies. 38pp. 5.50 x 5.50 inches.

This collection of poems was written on the occasion of the poet's twenty-fourth wedding anniversary and offered as a gift to his wife. A circle of particular intimacy has been drawn by these poems and their accompanying photographs – a circle inside of which languor lies entwined with both passion and risk.

6.
The Book of Silences
Robert Bringhurst. 2000.

The type is hand-set Meridien, printed letterpress in three colors on dampened handmade Moulin du Verger paper. The text is augmented by two hand-sensitized platinum photographs by Carolee

Campbell. The limp paper binding is handmade Renaissance V paper from the Barcham Green Hayle mill in England and Moulin du Verger handmade chaff paper. The enclosure is Renaissance III paper over boards and lined with handmade Japanese melon-vine paper. The photographs for this edition were printed by Gordon Mark in Santa Fe, New Mexico. The protective cases were assembled by Judi Conant in Guildhall, Vermont. Design, presswork, and binding are by Carolee Campbell, with binding assistance from Karen Skove Chu.

Edition of 100 numbered copies plus 12 *hors commerce*. 62 pp. 10.00 x 6.50 inches.

In this book of poems by Robert Bringhurst, the poet ruminates upon the nature of Zen Buddhist thought by turning over the stones of its history and pre-history, while echoing the voices of its philosopher-monks in his own poetic voice.

7.
The Architextures 1-7: "The Man of Music"
Nathaniel Tarn. 1998.

The type is hand set in Meridien with Felix Titling for the display, printed letterpress in six colors on dampened dove-gray abaca paper made for this edition by Katie MacGregor in Whiting, Maine. Six colored wood block embellishments augment the text throughout, beginning from the opening fly leaf, culminating in two double-page abstract illustrations and carrying through to the closing fly. The boards are covered inside and out in thin brass that has been alternately torched and patinated until a variety of colors bloom, making each book unique. The spine is made of both brass and stainless steel. The text is attached at the spine by a system of delicate brass rods passing through small stainless steel hinges, resulting in an integrated slender spine. The spine was originally developed by Daniel E. Kelm at his Wide Awake Garage in Easthampton, Massachusetts. The clamshell-style box is covered in black kyosei-shi, a handmade paper from the Fuji Paper Mills Cooperative in Tokushima, Japan. The box was assembled by Judi Conant in Guildhall, Vermont. The brass covers, as well as the wood block illustrations are by Carolee Campbell. Design, presswork, and binding are by Carolee Campbell at Ninja Press.

Edition of 65 copies. 32 pp. 11.25 x 8.25 inches.

These are the first seven from a collection of seventy prose poems in all.

"Anthropologist, editor, critic, and translator, Nathaniel Tarn is above all a poet. Poetry is the center of his personality and his activity. His work, in full growth, reveals a rich temperament, a remarkable linguistic inventiveness and a vision both original and universal."
—Octavio Paz

8.
The Real World of Manuel Córdova
W. S. Merwin. 1995.

The type is hand-set Samson Uncial printed letterpress in six colors on kakishibu, a persimmon-washed and smoked handmade paper from the Fuji Paper Mills Cooperative in Tokushima, Japan. The text which is housed in an accordion-style binding, may be unfolded and read in hand, stanza by stanza, or opened entirely to reveal all forty-three, fourteen-line stanzas. Fully extended, the book is fifteen feet long. The image of a river undulates alongside the poem while the setting of the poem itself mirrors the serpentine meanders of the river. The river is printed from photopolymer plates in five colors gradually intermingling one after another. The color shift is created by hand on each print by blending the two colors with a brayer. The book's enclosure is a heavy cream-colored raw flax sheet, hand-made at the Center for the Book Papermaking Facility at the University of Iowa. The enclosure is lined with kakishibu on which is printed a map of the world, the first to show the world's currents, drawn by Athanasius Kircher in 1665. The map is hand-tinted with pencil in five colors echoing the colors of the river. The enclosure is fastened with alum-tawed goatskin and bone. The book is housed in an acrylic slipcase. Design, presswork, hand-tinting, and binding are by Carolee Campbell, with binding assistance from Karen Skove Chu.

Edition of 160 numbered copies plus 18 *hors commerce*. 47 pp. 3.50 x 13.25 inches. Opens to 15 feet.

The Real World of Manuel Córdova *is based upon actual events in the life of Manuel Córdova-Rios (1887–1978) as told to F. Bruce Lamb and subsequently published under the title,* Wizard of the Upper Amazon.

"As a poet W. S. Merwin has charted a course that we, his first, marveling readers, might never have foreseen. From that early work, with its ravishing detours rich in echo and ornament, he has attained — more and more with every collection — a wonderful streamlined diction that unerringly separates and recombines like quicksilver scattered upon a shifting plane, but which remains as faithful to the warms and cools of the human heart as that same mercury in the pan-pipe of a thermometer."
—James Merrill

9.
El Sol y Los de Abajo
José Montoya. 1992.

The type is hand-set Spectrum with a large wooden typeface for the display, printed letterpress in three colors on Mohawk Superfine cover. The binding is in the accordion style. As the text is attached to the front cover only, the pages may be pulled away from the boards to stand on their own creating a screen-like effect. Drawings taken from the poet's sketchbooks cover the boards and are printed from magnesium plates on dampened handmade cogon grass paper from the Philippines. The drawings are augmented by hand painted embellishments on the covers. Drawings by the poet are within the text as well. Design, presswork, and binding are by Carolee Campbell.

Edition of 195 copies. 12 pp. 13.00 x 6.00 inches.

José Montoya has been one of the premiere cultural activists in the Chicano movement. He is an artist, a musician, and a poet. He writes in a linguistic braid of Spanish and English that exemplifies vividly the leap in perceptual and aesthetic power available to the bilingual poet. The language of the Chicano is more than a mixing of separate languages. It is a blend of the two into a third which becomes intrinsically fused – in other words, Spanish and English are no longer independent codes but a single hybrid. José Montoya is an expert in this linguistic synthesis.

10.
Mirror
Guillaume Apollinaire. 1986.

One double page opens to create a diptych which is bound in boards covered in handmade gray and black Japanese momo gami batik paper, giving the effect of a cracked and blacked mirror. The type is Perpetua, hand set in an elliptical shape in both French and English, and printed in three colors onto Crane's Artificial Parchment with silver reflective paper behind the text. Using cut and folded paper techniques by Carolee Campbell, the text opens to reveal a three-dimensional ellipse. Apollinaire's name is printed on the silver paper inside and behind the surrounding text, thus presenting the poem as it was originally written. The translation is by Anne Hyde Greet. Design, presswork, and binding are by Carolee Campbell.

Edition of 150 copies. 2pp. 8.00 x 4.25 inches.

Guillaume Apollinaire was a leading French poet and essayist of the early twentieth century. Included in his works were lyrical ideograms, poems designed to be printed with words arranged in pictorial forms. This edition of Mirror *is a three-dimensional rendition of the original as it appeared in* Calligrammes.

Peter Koch Printer

Peter Rutledge Koch got his start in printing in Missoula, Montana, when in a fit of under-employment back in 1974, he founded Black Stone Press and *Montana Gothic: A Journal of Poetry, Literature & Graphics*, publishing the art and writings of his friends in small editions. He immediately acquired a nineteenth-century Chandler and Price printing press and – together with his first wife, Shelley Hoyt – opened a letterpress printing office to pay the bills and provide endless amusement designing ephemera and art prints for the community of Montana artists and artisans. After four years of maverick literary production and self-instruction in typographic design in Missoula, Koch relocated the press in San Francisco and embarked on a one-year apprenticeship in book design with Adrian Wilson at his renowned Press in Tuscany Alley on Telegraph Hill in historic North Beach.

After the dissolution of Black Stone Press in 1983, Koch struck out on his own to publish under numerous imprints creatively named to suit different facets of his work: Peter Koch, Printers; Hormone Derange Editions; and Editions Koch. Under these various press names he has printed over a hundred books, hundreds of broadsides and fine art prints, and indeed countless ephemeral bits and shards. Today, the Koch studios in Berkeley are filled with his ever-increasing collections of books, paintings, prints, rare typefaces in wood and in metal, antique printing equipment, and a generous assortment of apprentices, assistants, associates, and friends.

The work of Koch's press has grown over the years to include a deep commitment to publishing ancient Greek philosophers in new poetic translations, visionary documents extracted from the Western landscape and native peoples, and contemporary artists and writers from all over the world, most of whom Koch counts as his friends.

Koch is often asked "How do you select the work you publish?" and the answer is usually a short paragraph or two about dreams, integrity, friendship, and meaning. When asked "How do you *sell* your books?" Koch has offered with a certain laconic gesture, "One book at a time."

His books and artworks have been the subject of solo exhibitions at the New York Public Library; the San Francisco Public Library; the Widener Library at Harvard University; the Yellowstone Art Museum in Billings, Montana; the University of Montana Art Museum; the Missoula Art Museum; and the Holter Museum of Art in Helena, Montana.

A dedicated bibliophile, Koch has collected a small library of books on the historic origins and practice of typography and printing, artist's books and private press books by friends and colleagues, and also books that document the art and exploration of Montana and the West. As a public extension of his knowledge and commitment to the bibliosphere, he has for the past twenty years taught the art and history of the book at The Bancroft Library at the University of California, Berkeley.

In 2005 Koch and his second wife, Susan Filter, created the CODEX Foundation to preserve and promote the fine arts of the book. He is currently the director of the biennial CODEX International Book Fair and Symposium, and the publisher of CODEX Editions.

1.
The Lost Journals of Sacajewea
Debra Magpie Earling. Photo-interventions by Peter Rutledge Koch. 2010.

The text is printed on Twinrocker Da Vinci handmade paper and bound at the press by Jonathan Gerken. The smoked buffalo rawhide cover paper was hand-made by Amanda Degener especially for this edition, at Cave Papers in Minneapolis, Minnesota. The spine is beaded with trade beads and decorated with .38 caliber cartridge cases. The images were prepared by Donald Farnsworth at Magnolia Editions and printed on Kozo handmade paper with the assistance of Jonathan Gerken and Tallulah Terryll. The typeface is a version of the historic Fell types assumed to be the work of Dutch punchcutter Dirck Voskens, and interpreted by Jonathan Hoefler in a conscious attempt to reproduce the imperfect image that the Fell types left on paper when printed in the eighteenth century. The Fell types have been described as "retaining a retrogressive old-style irregularity," which somehow seems appropriate, given our purpose here in this book.

Edition of 65 copies. 80 pp. 10.00 x 15.50 inches.

The Lost Journals of Sacajewea began as a collaborative project during the bicentennial of the Lewis and Clark expedition as a critical response to the celebratory afflatus that customarily surrounds such events. Debra Magpie Earling's narrative takes us behind the eyes and ears of a pregnant seventeen-year-old Indian girl traveling up the Missouri River with the Expedition of Discovery (sic) in 1804-1806. She is haunted by visions of a dark future - visions that materialized all too accurately: as the Frontier disappeared, the Real West burst upon the landscape like poisonous mushrooms after a forest fire. While Debra Magpie Earling concentrated on what remained unsaid in the historic record, I concentrated on what was recorded but here re-contextualized by my own dark vision of the civilization that the photographers were intending to promote.

2.
Watermark
Joseph Brodsky. 14 photogravures from photographs by Robert Morgan. Venice. 2006.

This edition of *Watermark* was conceived as a homage to the great Venetian printer Aldus Manutius and was printed in Venice in 2005. The text paper, made especially for the edition by Twinrocker Papermill, carries our own watermark inspired by Venetian Byzantine windows and designed by Christopher Stinehour and Susan Filter. Robert Morgan's photographs were digitally reconfigured by Donald Farnsworth and printed at Magnolia Editions in Oakland, California, from photogravure plates made by Unai San Martin. The printed sheets were shipped to Venice, where we printed the text in Monotype Dante cast in lead at the legendary Olivieri Typefoundry in Milan. Once the printing at the Scuola Grafica was completed, the sheets were shipped to our studio in Berkeley where the book was bound in richly pigmented Venetian-red papers made by hand at Cave Papers in Minneapolis, Minnesota. The book is housed in a portfolio box by John DeMerritt Bookbinders. Copies numbered I to V designate the deluxe edition bound in full vellum, housed in an ebony box with a bronze plate cast at the Valese foundry in Venice embedded in the case, and includes an extra suite of photogravures signed by the artist. Fifteen copies are designated h/c (*hors commerce*).

Edition of 50 copies. 80 pp. 11.00 x 16.50 inches.

Watermark is a series of lyrical meditations woven from the fabric of Venice in the late twentieth century ... meditations on time and beauty ... a looking-glass romance of a Russian poet-in-exile with a city that beguiled his eye.

In early September 2005, we loaded a printing press, on loan from the Tipoteca Italiana Fondazione printing museum in Cornuda, onto a barge and floated it down the Grand Canal to the Scuola Internazionale di Grafica Venezia, where I was artist-in-residence during Fall 2006. The making of this book was one of the most satisfying and elaborate adventures of my life mainly because a group of good friends, great printers in their own right, had volunteered to come to Venice and work with us: Christopher Stinehour and Jonathan Gerken from Berkeley, Russell Maret from New York, Karen Bleitz from London, and Jan & Crispin Elsted from Vancouver. Crispin set the final paragraph. It is enough to break your heart. It is one of the most beautiful pieces of Brodsky's prose that I can think of. It is about a tear, it's about time, it's about loss, and about beauty. Like the

Parmenides, Watermark *is a private-press book made with no concessions to the market ... it is a pure expression of the spirit of place and the esteem with which we hold our collaborators and friends.*

3.
Nature Morte
Peter Rutledge Koch. 2005.

This is a portfolio of digital pigment prints assembled from historic photographs and documents; the manuscript journals and papers of Meriwether Lewis, William Clark, and Elers Koch; selections from the writings of Ross Cox, William T. Horniday, L.A. Huffman, and others; and short legends by the artist. All texts have been set in lead type. A preface by Rick Newby, an introduction by Griff Williams, and a written statement by the artist complete the portfolio.

The images are printed on Hahnemühle Photo Rag by Urban Digital Color in San Francisco and the title engraving and texts are printed letterpress on Hahnemühle Copperplate by Peter Koch. The portfolio boxes are linen-paneled with a stamped quarter leather spine and made by John DeMerritt in Emeryville, California.

The portfolio consists of eleven images printed in a landscape format on sheets 16.00 x 22.00 inches and slipped into folios on which are printed the accompanying texts. The title page, documentation, and essays are printed on loose folios and housed with the images in a quarter-leather clamshell box. The title page collage/engraving was hand-colored at the press by Susan Filter.

Edition of 25 copies. 11 prints. 22.00 x 16.00 inches.
CROWBAIT exhibition print. 43.00 x 60.00 inches
DEADFALL exhibition print. 34.00 x 57.00 inches

Nature Morte *is my second experiment utilizing digital "photo-interventions" that I first developed in* Hard Words. *These prints were originally commissioned by the Holter Art Museum in Helena, Montana, for the* bicentennial of the Lewis and Clark expedition of 1804-1805. *The compounded images illustrate my vision/version of the natural history of disaster — the first death of the American West prompted by the aftermath of the expeditions of discovery and the subsequent death by civilization.*

4.
The Fragments of Parmenides & An English Translation by Robert Bringhurst
Wood engravings by Richard Wagener. 2004.

The text comprises twenty Greek fragments, varying in length from only a few words to sixty-six hexameters, of a poem composed by Parmenides almost 2,500 years ago in southern Italy. For this project, Koch commissioned Dan Carr to create a new typeface that balanced the lyricism and movement of the handwritten poem and the formality of a carefully-made inscription. Parmenides Greek, the foundry face designed, cut, and cast by Carr at the Golgonooza Letter Foundry, is accompanied by Diogenes Greek, a digital face designed by Christopher Stinehour. The text is printed in Greek on verso pages, with Bringhurst's translation on the facing recto pages. The Greek text was handset in Parmenides Greek at the press by Richard Seibert, Robert Bringhurst, and Peter Koch; the English text was set in Monotype Dante at the Golgonooza Letter Foundry; cover text, printed in red and black, was set in Diogenes Greek. Five wood engravings that boldly accent the text were hand-printed by Wagener in vibrant red, fiery orange and velvety black on Zerkall mill paper. 120 numbered copies, bound by Peggy Gotthold at Foolscap Press in quarter leather and Hahnemühle Bugra paper, are enclosed in a case covered in gold Japanese silk. Twenty-six lettered copies, bound in full leather by Daniel Kelm and enclosed in a drop-back box, are accompanied by a suite of ten wood engravings signed by Richard Wagener and a broadside specimen sheet for each of the typefaces made for this edition. Afterword by Bringhurst has been set in special digital Dante, New Hellenic Greek, and Lazurski Cyrillic, and printed from polymer plates.

Edition of 146 copies. 64 pp. 9.75 x 16.25 inches.

This volume is my third venture into the realm of ancient Greek philosophy. Here the intention is to publish a classically pure text in a brilliant poetic translation by one of the foremost poet-philosophers of our own civilization. The format is intended as an homage to the great printing tradition of private-press publishing where no effort is too much so long as the desired effect is achieved. Thus we have a new and original metal typeface commissioned for the Greek, the finest leather binding constructed for the lettered edition, and prints executed with the utmost exacting standards by the artist himself.

5.
Hard Words
Peter Rutledge Koch. Editions Koch/Gallery 16. 2000.

This features two large-scale exhibition prints from a suite of 15 images co-published and produced at Gallery 16 under the direction of Griff Williams. *Hard Words* was an early experiment in utilizing the (then) newest experimental digital printing methods to create images generated from scans of the original photoengravings and hand-set types in the collection of Peter Koch Printers. The images were digitally re-configured to produce densely pigment-saturated prints. They were printed on Somerset Radiant White 500 gsm, and mounted on wood.

Edition of 15 prints. HARD. 39.00 x 30.00 inches. DEAD. 26.00 x 46.00 inches.

These one-word picture poems were first begun in 1991 in an attempt to reformulate the custom of issuing "Wanted" posters. I was searching for a new language form to express what was wanting (wanted) in my own vocabulary of symbols. The lead and wood types, and copper electroplated and zinc photoengravings were collected from such various sources as a newspaper office near Freezout, Montana, and a printer's junkyard in San Francisco.

6.
Zebra Noise with a flatted seventh
Richard Wagener. 1998.

This abecedarium and bestiary was commissioned by Peter Koch from the artist Richard Wagener in 1991. It came to completion seven years later in what has been hailed *a tour de force* of wood engraving by a modern master. Designed and printed on Zerkall paper by Peter Koch and Richard Wagener, the text, twenty-six short fictions by Wagener, evokes the American West – a dry climate with black shadows. Accompanying the text are twenty-six wood engravings in black that follow the artist's zoological alphabet, from the armadillo, *Tolypeutes tricinctus*, to the meadow jumping mouse, *Zapus hudsonius*. In addition to the zoological alphabet blocks, there are twelve engravings in red that serve as backgrounds for the initial letters used to indicate a new section. The text is composed in Monotype Ehrhardt cast by the Golgonooza Letter Foundry. The binding is by Peggy Gotthold, using quarter leather and printed gray Fabriano Roma paper over boards, with gold lettering on the spine. The book is housed in a red cloth slipcase plus gray chemise.

Edition of 70 copies. 110 pp. 9.00 x 15.00 inches.

I first met Wagener in 1990 and was immediately struck by his enormous talent as an engraver and as an artist - two talents rarely found together in one individual. The maturity of his work was already apparent and I was astonished that he had not published books. I was eager to engage him in a project and images were swirling about in his work that begged to be brought under the ordered discipline of an abecedarium. This was the first of a series of collaborations that I have enjoyed with the artist.

7.
Ur-Text Volume 1
Peter Rutledge Koch. 1994.

The text is composed in Monotype Goudy Text and printed on Serpa hand-made paper watermarked with the press logo. The pages are hand-sewn onto alum-tawed goatskin thongs and covered in goatskin vellum, with twisted calfskin and Tibetan bone bead clasps. Various binders have contributed to the design and execution of the vellum treatment.

Edition of 26 copies. 248 pp. 4.25 x 6.50 inches.

Ur-Text, the concrete poem "Wordswords," is an icon in the form of a sacred text translated into a typographic form (see Ur-Text 3).

8.
Ur-Text Volume 2
Peter Rutledge Koch. Work-in-progress.

This volume consists of loose sheets in a portfolio, with letterpress printing in Remington Reproducing Bold and Goudy Text, and collage on Mohawk Superfine paper.

Sheet size: 11.00 x 17.00 inches (open).

This unique volume is intended as an illustrated "intellectual history" of the follies and a few triumphs attributed to Western man and the scientific mind of which we are so justly, or perhaps unjustly, proud. The images and marginalia are misleading and deliberately occulted by their fragmentary nature, producing an apocalyptic vision dominated by the book's iconic structure.

9.
Ur-Text Volume 3
Peter Rutledge Koch 1994.

The text is composed in Monotype Reproducing Bold type and printed on Mohawk Superfine paper. The binding is by Daniel Kelm in various metals, and is done by hand. Covers are acid-etched zinc lined with doublures of oxidized brass. Primary sewing is braided dacron thread holding each signature to an external brass spine rod covered by aluminum tube segments, leaving space for a weaving of braided silk thread which connects the covers and signatures. The volume is housed in a black and red Japanese-cloth-covered portfolio with magnetic fore-edge flap. Page edges are tinted black.

Edition of 26 copies. 92 pp. 10.50 x 16.00 inches.

This hyper-modernist and final edition of the concrete poem "Wordswords" is my symbolic final disarticulation following a temporary loss of faith in The Word. The poem/text was originally composed as a contribution to a graduate metaphysics seminar and subsequently occasioned my departure from pursuing further graduate philosophical studies at the University of Montana back in 1970. Ur-Text is an extreme example of a metaphor and icon of the "book as object." The book has the distinction of being continually misunderstood, harshly judged, and even rejected from an exhibition of illustrated artists' books based on a curator's decision that the book was not illustrated. My argument that the book is an icon and therefore a picture of a book went unheeded.

10.
Diogenes: Defictions
Peter Rutledge Koch. Text: Thomas McEvilley. Ceramic box: Stephen Braun. 1994.

This "text transmission object" is a collaborative sculpture designed as a "forgery" of a hypothetical object discovered by archeologists in the dump of ancient Corinth where Diogenes was presumed to live. The text was hand-lettered by Christopher Stinehour and printed letterpress from zinc engravings onto lead tablets by Koch. The "defixiones" are housed loose in a glazed ceramic box by the sculptor Stephen Braun; each box is unique in color and shape. The text, a selection of twenty-one selected short, philosophical performance pieces by Thomas McEvilley, was translated from the lore surrounding the proto-cynic Diogenes of Sinope. As the plates are loose and unpaginated, they can be read in a random order.

Edition of 50 copies. 11 tablets 5.00 x 7.00 inches.

This collaboration, the second in my Greek series, has been a source of constant wonder. It has been received in the art world as sculpture, in the book world as an artist's book, in the household as a conversation piece, and in the marketplace as an "object d'art." Diogenes would have been amused, I'm certain.

11.
Point Lobos
Robinson Jeffers. Photographs by Wolf von dem Bussche. Introduction by William Everson. Edited by Peter Rutledge Koch. Oakland, California: Peter and the Wolf Editions. 1987.

Point Lobos is an homage to the place and to the poet Robinson Jeffers. Hailed as a masterwork and one of the great printed works of the late twentieth century, *Point Lobos* is a collaboration between the typographer and printer Peter Rutledge Koch, and the photographer Wolf von dem Bussche. The text comprises fifteen poems by Jeffers, chosen for their various reverberations of the spirit and beauty of Point Lobos, and a lengthy introduction by William Everson, the poet, printer, and Jeffers scholar. The poems are hand set in Albertus and Pegasus types; the introduction and colophon are set in Monotype Van Dijck, and printing is by Peter Koch on Rives BFK White, with the publisher's device embossed on the lower right-hand corner of each leaf. The title page is printed in terra cotta and black. Fifteen original photographs by von dem Bussche dramatically mirror the text and document the site of Jeffers' inspiration. The pages are housed loose in a special folding case covered in German linen made by Klaus-Ullrich Rötzscher. A custom slipcase is handcrafted from three-quarter inch black walnut by Shigoto Ya, Inc.

Edition of 125 copies (52 of which were destroyed in the Oakland firestorm of 1991).
Portfolio: 42 prints, 18.00 x 22.00 inches.

In 1985 Wolf von dem Bussche and I were trout fishing in the Sierra Nevada. I was demonstrating a difficult under-the-bush cast early in the evening when I casually remarked that one of my favorite poets was Robinson Jeffers. Wolf immediately responded that he shared my enthusiasm and that he had photographed Point Lobos for the Time Life series on the art and history of photography. I knew immediately that we had a project. Wolf is an extremely gifted photographer and his dark vision matched Jeffers' own. This was an exciting adventure from start to finish. The unfortunate part of this most fortunate collaboration is that so many copies were destroyed by fire, thereby reducing the size of the edition to seventy-three copies.

Turkey Press · Edition Reese

Harry Reese established Turkey Press in 1974, when he was a graduate student at Brown University. He moved to Berkeley, California, in 1975 where he met Sandra Liddell Paulson who was teaching in the San Francisco Unified School District by day, and serving cocktails at the St. Francis Hotel by night. In 1977 they moved from Berkeley to Isla Vista, where they married, bought a house, and became equal partners in Turkey Press. Initially a publisher of poetry books in small-press limited editions, Turkey Press started small and got smaller, as its proprietors learned how art and teaching fitted into, and shaped, their own lives.

Paths of exploration in their work continually open up for them because in their own respective ways they have both wanted the freedom to control the means of production. They design, print from metal types and unconventional plates and surfaces on a Vandercook press, make paper from cloth and natural fibers, and bind each edition, in which their own visual art is often included. The design and production of Turkey Press books is a weaving process. One of the two partners usually ends up doing either more or less than the other. Because they both feel completely responsible for the work, they share equally in the outcome, regardless of who thought about it first or who eventually performed a specific task. Dialogue dictates and translates experience: visual, literary, technical. Front and back, back and forth, the book emerges.

In 1990 they created Edition Reese, an imprint for more eccentric, individual, and collaborative artists' books that provides them opportunities to engage with provocative thinkers and to work with a range of new and old technologies available to artists today. Edition Reese has produced twelve limited edition titles, all of which include original art and distinctive bindings. As of 2011 Turkey Press has issued 57 books, primarily contemporary poetry in a variety of formats and edition sizes.

Harry Reese and Sandra Liddell Reese have received their share of recognition, including grants and awards from the National Endowment for the Arts, the California Arts Council, and the American Institute for Graphic Arts. Having taught since 1978 at the University of California, Santa Barbara (UCSB), Harry Reese is a professor in the department of art and associate dean of the College of Creative Studies. An occasional part-time instructor in hand papermaking and book arts classes at UCSB, Sandra Liddell Reese has directed her full attention over the last three decades to the work of Turkey Press. The Turkey Press archives were acquired by the Getty Center for the History of Art and the Humanities (now the Getty Research Institute) in 1992.

1.

33 1/3: Off the Record

Harry Reese. Edition Reese (Isla Vista) and Alpha Presse (Frankfurt, Germany). 1995-2009.

This artist's book was initiated in 1995 by Harry Reese – using his prints, drawings, painting, and typography – to celebrate the tenth anniversary of Alpha Presse, a publisher of limited edition artists' books in Frankfurt, Germany. Along the way he samples Cyrano de Bergerac, Thomas Edison, and, most importantly, Marshall McLuhan, who understood that each new medium has the capacity to contain or express all other mediums. This work utilizes 33 1/3 vinyl long-play records as the matrix for the artwork. After showing this project at the 2007 Codex Book Fair, we decided to revise the edition to incorporate new and different prints, and to show a more integrated sequential page display that features the reverse side of each sheet as part of a double-page spread. The book design includes an exhibition-style binding, produced by Sandra Liddell Reese, that allows for individual pages to be taken out of the book structure and displayed. Additional images, texts and prints, along with Sandra's redesign of the original format, were made as recently as 2009 to round out the edition.

Edition of 12 copies. 16.50 x 17.25 inches.

—From the book:
"I come from a musical family. My sister played the violin. My uncle sang in the opera. My father played the radio. And I played with records."
    – Harry Reese

"The new technology turns the old technology into an art form."
    – Marshall McLuhan

2.
The Sea Gazer
Michael Hannon. Cut paper illustration by Harry Reese. Turkey Press. 2007.

The images for this long poem were originally created for a unique artist's book by Harry Reese in 2003. The type is hand-set Dante printed on dampened Hahnemühle Biblio. The images for this edition, based on scans from the 2003 book, were cut on a Roland plotter from sheets of adhesive-backed kitakata. Overall monoprints from plexiglass in solid orange and black ink, and monoprints from a wood grain block were printed on the kitakata before it was cut. The paper used for the spine and cover was hand-made by Sandra Liddell Reese and inkjet printed on an Epson 4800 with the image of a scanned monotype by Harry Reese.

Edition of 75 copies. 26 pages. 9.25 x 14.50 inches.

From the announcement of the unique artist's book in 2003:
"Twenty-five years ago I read "The Sea Gazer," a poem that Michael Hannon wrote in 1964 and initially had published in City Lights Journal, No. 3, in San Francisco in 1966. It was the basis of our first publication of Michael Hannon's poetry in 1978, Ship Without Paper. Since that time Sandra and I have published five books and many broadsides and cards that feature Michael's work. I have included lines from his poems in paintings and prints I have made. He wrote "poetic" commentary to accompany a

show of paintings, Imaginary Lyrics, I had in 1995. The poet Brooks Roddan has acutely observed that Michael Hannon's poems operate "between the poles of surrender and struggle." Michael Hannon's poetry has held me in its sway ever since I met and published him."

3.
Kinnikinnick Brand Kickapoo Joy-Juice
Jonathan Williams. Drawings of Kilpeck Church by John Furnival. Monoprints and typographic drawing by Sandra Liddell Reese. Turkey Press. 2004.

In this volume are seventy-six power-packed gulps of quintessential Jonathan Williams (1929-2008), in the form of meta-fours (four-word-per-line poems of undetermined length) in combination with pen and ink drawings by John Furnival of the doorway and carved tympanum and corbels from the church of St Mary's and St David's in the village of Kilpeck in Herefordshire, England. Transparent ink was applied through a stencil to the text pages in a thick layer to create a honey-colored ground on top of which the images were printed from polymer plates. The type is Narrow Bembo and Gill Sans cast by the Letterfoundry of Michael and Winifred Bixler and printed on 100 pound Dulcet. Copies were bound in a hybrid false-accordion, sewn-boards style using handmade paper on the spine and cover from the Oakdale Paper Facility at the University of Iowa. The color of the cover paper was changed substantially through hand application of acrylic paint to achieve its present 'joy-juice' vibrancy.

Edition of 145 copies. 48 pages. 4 x 10.5 inches.

It was R. Buckminster Fuller who remarked of Jonathan Williams that "he is our Johnny Appleseed – we need him more than we know." Educated at St. Albans School, Princeton, and Black Mountain College, he once listed his occupations as "poet, publisher, designer, essayist, iconographer." Quoting Jonathan Williams: "I have a mind like a blue darter (a kind of Appalachian lizard – I don't have a lizard book at hand and can't give you the proper Latin formalities). The point is: if you don't take a rip, you won't do diddly. So there'll be lots of frozen ropes, an occasional long tater, and even the odd tall can of corn. Guys like the Babe and Hammerin' Harmon Killebrew struck out more than all the others, just to hit the big one. That suits me just fine."

4.
Grasshopper
Paloma Cain, Jonathan Cecil, Harry Reese. Edition Reese. 2000.

This is an artist's book, the result of collaboration between Paloma Cain, Jonathan Cecil and Harry Reese. Our large format book includes oil-based monotype prints, letterpress printing, scanned images and computer-generated text with laser print and ink jet output on Monadnock Dulcet text paper in a variation of the sewn-boards binding. Paloma Cain and Jonathan Cecil hand-inked and printed the multilayered monotypes that were unique in each boxed set. The cover photo was by Harry Reese.

Edition of 30 copies. 12.00 x 15.00 inches.

The text combines fragments and scans from versions of the I Ching – the Princeton University Wilhelm/Baynes translation and Thomas Meyer's previously unpublished translation – with excerpts from Philip K. Dick's novel, The Man in the High Castle. Philip K. Dick (1928-1982) wrote novels, short stories, and essays almost exclusively in the science fiction genre. The Man in the High Castle bridged the genres of alternate history and science fiction, and it received the Hugo Award for Best Novel in 1963.

An accomplished poet and innovative translator, who taught himself Chinese using FileMaker Pro, Thomas Meyer was the constant companion and editorial amanuensis of Jonathan Williams at the Jargon Society for over thirty years. Flood Editions published his complete translation of the Chinese classic, Dao De Jing, an imagistic version arranged in couplets in 2005.

5.
The Standard
Harry Reese. Edition Reese. 1997.

Conceptually designed by Sandra Liddell Reese, the poem has been recontextualized within a faux gold brick with a Victor-brand rat trap set into the inside cover of each drop-spine box. The type is hand-set Times New Roman and Franklin Gothic printed on MacGregor handmade paper. The poem and drawings are displayed across a four panel accordion fold format. Each slim volume is bound in the reclaimed leather doublure lining from the disintegrating covers of the 11th edition of the *Encyclopedia Britannica* and is contained within the gold brick box.

Edition of 26 copies. 5.00 x 11.00 x 4.00 inches.

Harry Reese's poem "The Standard," written while he was a graduate student in the Creative Writing Program at Brown University and published in a limited edition in 1975 by Turkey Press titled Unknown Friends, ends with a coruscating invective about the nature of hoardable commodities. During the 1996 presidential campaign Al Gore attended a luncheon at a Buddhist temple after which over 50,000 dollars in illegal campaign contributions were received by the Democratic National Committee through the monks and nuns who made contributions in their own names and were then reimbursed by the temple from its general funds. Gore's Orwellian defense of his attendance at this event, "I sure as hell did not have any conversation with anyone saying this is a fundraising event," that it was instead "community outreach" and "donor maintenance," provided the provocation for a theatrical display of this satirical poem.

In contrast to most of our work this book is a maximalist display of materials. It may be the only instance that a rat trap has been presented so reverently surrounded by gold paper that one can study its efficient killing mechanism perched on the pristine letterpressed image of a mouse head that fills the counter of the V in the registered Victor brand logo. We rescued a complete set of the eleventh edition of the Encyclopedia Britannica *from* a small college that wanted to be rid of it because of the undesirable smell of the suede covers. I re-covered the set with paper wrappers and was able to reclaim the inner side of the smelly leather for its new purpose as cover for a poem about dead rats. A physicist friend guessed correctly that lead, used in a hidden compartment to simulate the weightiness of a gold brick, was the only metal we could have used with sufficient weight and for low cost. Maybe in some future time rats will gnaw away the gold foil to discover another hidden text of metal.

6.

Funagainstawake
Harry Reese. New York: Granary Books. 1997.

In *Finnegans Wake* there are ten one-hundred-letter words that have been referred to (by Joyce and others) as thunderclaps or thunders. Our title, *Funagainstawake*, plays on the satirical intent of the novel in which language is used inventively to entertain and wake up its readers. The "ten thunders" operate as both source material and titles for the artist's series of ten monotypes, or unique prints, in each book. The images were painted on flexible vinyl sheets and printed on Magnani Italia paper. One of the printed vinyl plates from the series has been mounted on each title page. The edition of thirty copies (with two artist's proofs) was bound at the Wide Awake Garage by Daniel E. Kelm and staff using the wire-edge hinging structure. Featuring all the ten thunders, each typographic cover was letterpress printed, hand painted, bordered by cloth, and mounted on board. The type is Perpetua. Jill Jevne made the cloth-covered boxes.

Edition of 32 copies. 12.00 x 9.00 inches

"*Fun against awake. Entertainment versus enlightenment. Having fun. Waking up. The artist invents the means to bridge biological inheritance and the environment created by technological innovation. Fun again, stay awake.*

"*I am concerned now, as was James Joyce in his time, with issues of how human beings are shaped by their technologies. Anyone who has tried to "read" this book in a conventional way knows that it is extremely difficult, perhaps impossible, to read. Today, over fifty years after its publication, Finnegans Wake is more ignored than discussed and much more discussed than read. As a difficult text that is talked about for its form and techniques, rather than read discursively or linearly for information, Finnegans Wake can be considered in some of the same ways that contemporary visual art has been theorized and discussed. It has much affinity with, and similarity to, a contemporary artist's book.*"
—*Unpublished notes by Harry Reese, 1997*

7.

Heart Island and Other Epigrams
James Laughlin. Turkey Press. 1996.

Included here are forty-four short poems by James Laughlin (1914-1997), the founding publisher of New Directions, in 1936. Composition is in Walbaum by the Letterfoundry of Michael & Winifred Bixler, and printing is on dampened Nideggen. Wood engravings by M. L. Breton from the *Dictionnaire Infernal* (Paris, 1818) were printed letterpress from polymer plates on French folded Kitakata. All was hardbound in linen with a hand-colored image on each cover panel.

Edition of 200 copies. 76 pages. 5.00 x 8.25 inches

In 1983 Sandra and Harry Reese were introduced to James Laughlin by David D. Cooper, not only the oldest friend of Turkey Press but a highly regarded scholar on the work of Thomas Merton. The strong connection between Cooper and Laughlin would eventually lead to Turkey Press's publication in 1988 of The Alaskan Journal, at the time one of the few remaining unedited and unpublished works of the late Thomas Merton. The Reeses engaged in an extended dialogue and correspondence with Laughlin on the matter of how poetry comes from the mind and voice to the page. As a student at Harvard in the 1930's, Laughlin had found a poetic style he would use the rest of his life, in which each succeeding line could vary from the typewriter length of the first line by no more than one space either way, or - in rare emergencies - two spaces.

In 1985, Turkey Press published Stolen and Contaminated Poems, a collection of twenty-four previously unpublished poems by Laughlin, followed by a section of anecdotal jottings about them. In an essay about Laughlin, Stephen Kessler writes: "He not only pretended to have become a publisher due to his failure as a would-be poet, but he kept his practice and increasing skill and depth as a writer of verse pretty much out of sight until the last years of his life, revealing what [Eliot] Weinberger called 'one of the secret treasures of American poetry.'"

8.
RE
Kiki Smith. Text adapted from John A. Wilson's translation of an Egyptian cosmology. Edition Reese. 1994.

Three photographic images of the artist were printed from a photoengraving on Whatman paper showing a 1954 watermark, the year the artist was born. The text was letterpress printed from hand-set Palatino. Gampi silk tissue is adhered to the edge of the eight-fold format allowing for a sculptural display of text and image.

Edition of 100 copies contained in a paper envelope. 7.00 x 9.00 inches.

Kiki Smith is best known as a visual artist whose work addresses the human body - simultaneously so frail and so enduring - and whose medium over the years has included glass, plaster, ceramics, bronze and paper. Smith's passion for communal environments has driven her to create much of her work in collaborative settings. While her one-person exhibit – Kiki Smith: A Sojourn in Santa Barbara – was at UC Santa Barbara's University Art Museum in 1994, curator Elizabeth Brown proposed a collaborative print or book project with Turkey Press.

We discussed several formats for presenting her photographic imagery along with the text. She eventually chose the eight-fold book - a single sheet cut and folded, creating eight page surfaces - with the additional request that we attach a sheet of gampi silk tissue to the edge of the folded sheet, almost like a skirt. In an interview with Carlo McCormick for the Journal of Contemporary Art, Smith said, "I made things out of bronze for a while, but I really like making things delicate. I guess you could call them 'girls' materials, but they're just things associated with girls. In making work that's about the body I'm always playing between the two extremes of life: this ferocious force that keeps propelling us and at the same time how you can just pierce it and it dies. My paper sculptures are made out of paper that is used for archival purposes and is very tough and strong. It's a little bit deceiving because it looks more fragile than it really is."

Smith is instinctively drawn to the concept of repetition, which is so intimately interwoven with printmaking. "It's about repetition versus uniqueness. Prints mimic what we are as humans: we are all the same and yet everyone is different."

9.
Arplines
Harry Reese. Turkey Press. 1990.

Drawings, relief prints, collages, typographic prints, paintings, and collaged poems by Harry Reese are based on the work of Jean (Hans) Arp, whose work inspired this portfolio. Text lines from Arp's poems, letters, interviews, prose writings, and experiences were lifted from their original contexts, worked over, translated at times, and then recombined with various new images and objects to make new poems. "The lines are Arp's, but the poems are mine," declares the appropriator/author/artist/publisher. Various hand-set types were used, including Times New Roman, News Gothic, Franklin Gothic, Perpetua, wood type, and some unnamed found types. A chemise wrapper of Japanese tea-chest paper with shapes cut out by hand contains the loose laid sheets in each boxed set. Binding is by Sandra Liddell Reese, with help from Dawn Koncsol. Including the title page and signed colophon on a single three-part panel, the book consists of ten folded sheets with images and text. An original acrylic painting covers each clamshell box.

Edition of 43 copies, produced from 1989 to 1992. 8.00 x 13.00 inches.

Renée and Judd Hubert wrote about our work in several different publications, and their commentary in The Cutting Edge of Reading about a group of artist books, including Arplines, expresses very well for us how we approach our work, especially the projects of the last twenty years: "The artist book, however disruptive of tradition, strives for cohesion among its constituent parts by giving equal status to images, typography, binding, page-setting, folds, collages, and text. The reader must search, if not necessarily for perfect coherence, at least for a unifying purpose, within and outside the text."

10.
Turnings
Joan Tanner. Edition Reese. 1990.

The artist's writing has been typographically shaped and printed letterpress from hand-set Optima, Copperplate, Franklin Gothic and Headline Gothic, on dampened Turkey Press handmade paper. Three original drawings – one on sandpaper, one on carbon paper, and one in pencil onto discarded handmade paper proof sheets – are included in a sixteen-page signature. A portion of the text has been hand-stamped into the paper from metal punches. A four-panel fold-out portfolio contains an original painting – on a 10.00 x 15.00 inch birch panel in its specific box – as well as the letterpress-printed folio, which has been sewn and inserted into the lining of the portfolio.

A video documenting this two-year-long collaboration was filmed in the studios of the artist and the publisher by Wayne McCall and Associates, and it marks the first publication of the Edition Reese imprint, established to provide a forum for collaborative projects between artists. This video has now been combined on a DVD with an electronic catalogue of all the individual artwork for this entire project, which as part of the original design for *Turnings* was inset into the clamshell box that protects the work.

Edition of 20 copies. 12.75 x 17.75 inches.

Joan Tanner's art is predicated upon many of the elements that characterize written and spoken language: structure, syntax, morphology, symbol, classification, and communication. Both her verbal and visual investigations seem effortless in the end but are the result of an often complex journey that makes its way through her multiple interests in theater, linguistics, phenomenology, "outsider" art, ophthalmology, film, the poetry and radio plays of Samuel Beckett, plant life, architecture and early Renaissance painting, to name a few. Her sensitivity to materials and her commitment to the manual activity of making art (what she frequently refers to as "handedness") are paramount. Tanner's near-reverence for the literal past of the materials she uses to make her art demonstrates a trail of evidence, of both her physical process and her decision making.

Tanner believes that "In order to restore vision and the connoisseurship of looking at color and shape, particularly the translucency of paint on top of a panel of wood, the viewer must have the ability to hold a surface like a musical score, move it, turn it, and then put it away." Because of the artist's hermetic urge to keep the viewer away from the constancy of viewing, we settled on a format that allowed for a kind of reading that had something to do with containment, requiring a curatorial effort on the part of the beholder – to move away from what would be encountered in a typical gallery situation.

Typography is ordinarily in the service of another goal and not thought of as an end in itself. We tend to think of it as an aid for the revelation of text. Joan Tanner's text had a subliminal or sub-textual element that needed some release and our role as Socratic midwife was to bring that about, to give some sort of sculpted shape to the breath.

11.
Fables
Michael Hannon. Drawings by William T. Wiley. Turkey Press. 1988.

Ten short poems, each in response to a poem title, were printed on Fuji Mill handmade kozo from hand-set Spectrum, Neuland,

and Albertus. The books were bound with help from Dawn Koncsol, using kakishibu on the front and back covers, and they were enclosed in a painted cloth clamshell box. The paper on the cover, with its particularly beautiful variegated surface, turned out to be a unique occurrence at the mill during the process of coating the kozo paper with natural persimmon dye. During a visit to our studio, the owner of Fuji Mill, in the company of Hiromi Katayama, the primary distributor of Japanese papers in the US, told us that *Fables* is the first western-style book in which Fuji Mill's papers were used.

Edition of 125 copies. 68 pages. 9.00 x 12.00 inches.

Having published the poetry of Michael Hannon since 1978, we believe that he is one of the best poets writing today. He started work on this collection in 1979 as a series of children's poems for his youngest son. In 1983 he and Wiley were introduced to each other through their mutual friend and poet, William Witherup (now deceased). After their meeting, Hannon sent Wiley a copy of Venerations and Fables, his 1982 book of poems from Turkey Press. Wiley produced a series of individual sculptures and drawings based on these fables, thus initiating a series of many (and various) collaborations between the poet and the artist. According to Hannon, Wiley's drawings are the "poem between the lines."

12.

Five Meters of Poems
Carlos Oquendo de Amat. Translated by David M. Guss. Woodcuts by Antonio Frasconi. Turkey Press. 1986.

In 1927, 5 Metros de Poemas was first published in Lima, Peru. This edition – the first time the entire book appears in English – consists of eighteen typographically playful poems in a visual sequence of accordion-folded panels, measuring five meters long when fully extended. Our typographic design was based on one of only three extant copies in the United States, held in the Bancroft Library at UC Berkeley. Three hundred copies were printed on Mohawk

Superfine cover from handset Goudy Modern, Underwood Typewriter, and other assorted types and bound in printed BFK Rives over thin board. Forty deluxe copies, signed by the translator and the artist, were printed on Barcham Green handmade India Office. A typographic print by Harry Reese, weaving the title of the book and the name of the poet, was printed on his handmade paper for the cover of the deluxe box.

Edition of 340 copies. 10.50 x 8.5 inches.

The decision to hand set, print and bind over three hundred copies was based partly on the acceptance speech of Mario Vargas Llosa for the Romulo Gallegos Literary Prize in Caracas in 1976, when he spoke about Oquendo de Amat and his oblivion:

"It wouldn't surprise me at all if the mice had come across the copies of his only book, buried in the libraries that no one visits, or if his poems that no one reads anymore become 'dust, wind, nothing,' like the insolent red shirt which he bought to die in. And yet, this countryman of mine was a consummate sorcerer, a witch with a word, a daring architect of images, a blazing explorer of dreams – a complete and obstinate creator who possessed the lucidity and the madness necessary to assume his vocation of a writer as it must be done, as one must do it: as a daily and furious immolation."

We met Antonio Frasconi – one of the most principled, compassionate, and exemplary artists of his generation – through a mutual friend during the summer when he and his wife, Leona Price (a fifth-generation Santa Barbaran), came to stay in her family home. We told him what we knew about Oquendo de Amat and his only book, and without any demands he agreed to contribute his work for the cover and opening pages of this edition.

Foolscap Press

LAWRENCE G. VAN VELZER & PEGGY GOTTHOLD
Santa Cruz

Foolscap Press brings together the talents of Lawrence G. Van Velzer and Peggy Gotthold, whose complementary backgrounds strengthen the production of their books. Their combined experiences in creative writing, literature, drawing, printmaking, carpentry, puppetry, bookbinding, and printing inform their choices of text and the strong sense that books are akin to performance. Foolscap books demonstrate an abiding interest in a well-told story or philosophy, and in each book the text is enhanced by historical or newly conceived visual elements.

Van Velzer and Gotthold also explore the possibilities in the synthesis of old forms re-imagined in new packages, as exemplified by four books on display: *The Tower of the Winds*, a scroll whose form was chosen because the content unrolls as a meditation on time and through history; *Other Worlds: Journey to the Moon*, where the text opens doors to a different understanding of imaginative travel; *Direction of the Road*, where an anamorphic woodcut asks the viewer and reader to bend time and perception; and *Herakles and the Eurystheusian Twelve-Step Program*, a retelling of Greek myths as a book and as a shadow-puppet movie.

Whatever ... out the sudden violent
so over ... dn't know if he/they had
... lings for his/their herds-
... for
... ay.

... iring

... he
... erally

... s
... ails
... get,
... he
... ttle

... y
... at
... s
... appy
... asn't

... d to
... ther

... d to
... s a
... all
... the
... is
... of
... h

Puppets used in the shadow-puppet movie.

Herakles and the Eurystheusian Twelve-Step Program.

I'm Working

Journal Entry
16 July 1988
Kainkordu Village, Sierra Leone, West Africa

Throughout the week I have been walking all over the village looking and listening as life composes itself all around me. It is very, very interesting. I am trying to remain as unobtrusive as possible though it is hard to do so. While photographing I have, at times, heard from behind me, some rustling and giggling. Turning quickly I have only managed to see the backsides of some local children as they scatter. Today, I was having a very productive day when again I heard something behind me. I turned to see four little boys perfectly posed with makeshift weed circles being held up to their eyes. They were turning the circles as I turned my lens to focus and I realized they were imitating me. I quickly took their picture and they then made a sound of a click as if taking my picture. I held back my smile and said, "Hey boys I'm working." Almost on cue they looked at each other and yelled back, "I'm working." With that I broke into laughter. The little boys continued to look through their makeshift lenses. We spent the rest of the day walking around the village together and me letting them look through my cameras. A good day.

Quick Change

Journal Entry
23 October 2006
Tangier, Morocco

The taxi driver has made his way through the city of 650,000 in short order, and dropped us at the fancy Tangier Ville train station. We are early and the station is nearly empty and quiet. The marble interior with its high ceiling is very grand and has a kind of mosque quality, which the silence of the place reiterates. While we are settling into two of the chairs in the center of the great room a man with taps on the heels of his shoes is walking across the stone floor and the sound of his metallic steps echoes off the walls. Like so much of Morocco I like this place but I really can't say why. Over the next hour the station begins to fill and all kinds of characters come and go. Outside a verbal fight has begun between a taxi driver and a policeman that seems to be about parking. They are just inches from each other's face as they yell and now others are gathering around them offering some views of their own. Making the scene even more entertaining is a man struggling through the arguing crowd balancing a giant stuffed panda bear in one hand while holding a little girl in the other. The policeman and the taxi driver are still yelling and now there are hand

I had so loved the morning that without really thinking I reached into my pocket and took out my Swiss army knife and placed it in Michael's hand and held it there for some time. He opened the knife and slowly cut a piece of cheese, which he handed to me. For a moment he just looked out over the valley and then put his hand on his heart and then touched my chest. I didn't know him when we hiked up to this place but I did now. I think I even loved him.

The stranger rolled another cigarette and sat in a chair near me. He produced a bottle of something, looked over and made some gesture of hello and offered me a drink. I accepted and nodded a thank you, he just smiled. I could see more clearly now the heavy lines on his face and his clear green eyes. Yes, his face was world-weary but the afternoon was beautiful and the drink in the bottle, while not lemon water, was delicious. I thought of Uncle Michael and I sitting together looking out over the valley as the stranger and I now sat watching the last of the sun moving toward its rest into the sea.

Despatches

Following page:
Direction of the Road

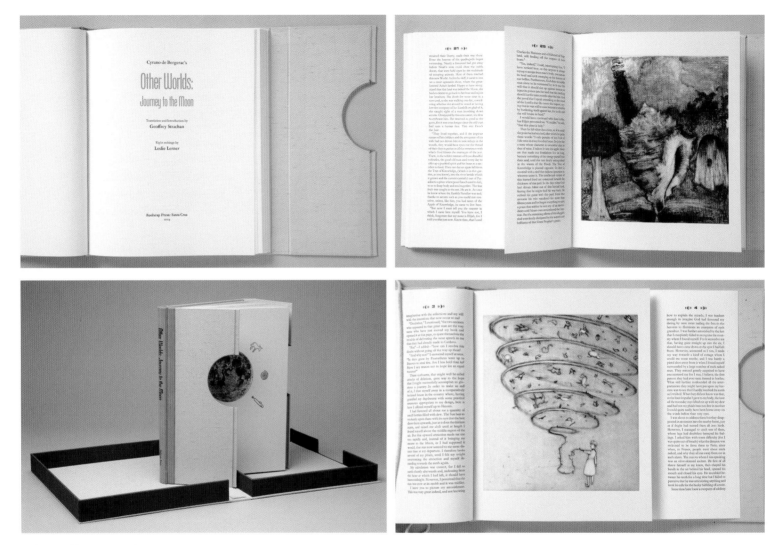

Other Worlds: Journey to the Moon

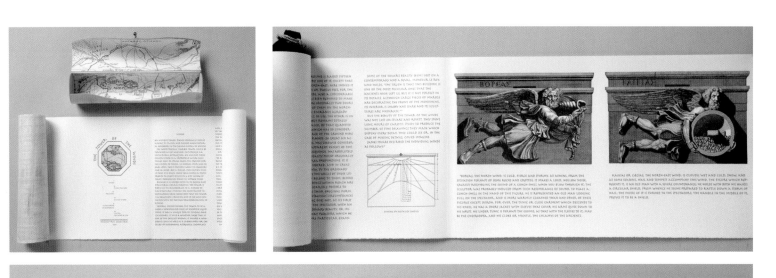

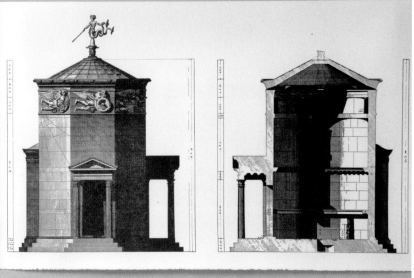

The Tower of the Winds

Crawfoot watched helplessly as the enormous snake positioned herself on the thick limb that stuck out directly over him.

"What a wonderful, pleasant surprise," hissed the snake, "to have a visitor such as yourself. My, my, my."

Crawfoot didn't like this situation at all—especially the 'My, my, my' part. From what he could see of the snake, she was quite thick around the middle. The kind of diner who is generally disappointed with skimpy meals. Most likely the kind who would probably say, 'Oh, one more helping of crow? Oh, I don't

mind if I do, thank you very much'. Crawfoot tried jerking and twisting in the mud, to somehow pull himself away from under the hazardous, low-lying branch. But all he could manage was to turn in a slow circle.

"Don't bother wearing yourself out," hissed the snake, whose large head was now directly over him. "Oh, you are a fat one. My, my, my, although *feathers* are not my favorite."

The snake gathered herself out on the limb and now gently lowered her head down to the pool. She would easily be able to reach Crawfoot. The thought of the snake's terrible face being so close made the crow shudder. Perhaps he could keep her away with loud and annoying noises.

"CAW! CAW! CAW!"

"What's that, the dinner bell?" joked the snake. Then she laughed. "Sissst, sisst, sisst." It was the most disgusting laugh imaginable.

When the snake was only a few inches from the crow, Crawfoot beat his wings on the surface of the muddy pool, sending a spray of mud directly into her face and eyes.

"Sisst!" She twisted in the air and swung her heavy head. She was surprised, but not discouraged. Her yellow eyes were protected by transparent lids.

Crawfoot tried it again, but he had no more lucky shots flinging mud.

77

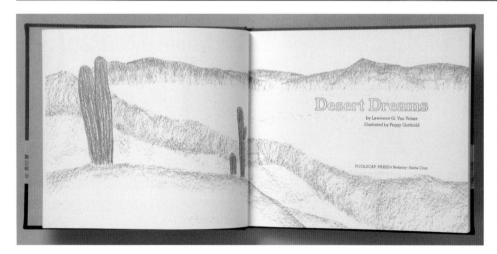

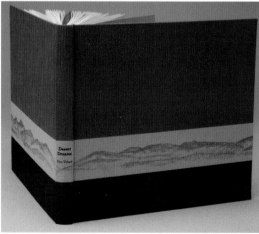

Desert Dreams

Moving Parts Press

FELICIA RICE
Santa Cruz

Felicia Rice arrived in Santa Cruz in 1974 to study with renowned San Francisco printer Jack Stauffacher and to apprentice with poet/printer William Everson at the University of California, Santa Cruz. By 1977 she had set Moving Parts Press in motion.

Her work has been fueled by political, socio-cultural, and historical commitment. Motivated to undertake nontraditional women's work and gain access to the power of the press, she learned to hang sheet rock, rebuild a VW engine, operate offset presses, hand set type, maintain a hot lead type-casting machine, run a variety of old style letterpresses, and publish books of contemporary art and literature.

Rice has one foot firmly planted in the 19th -century and the other in the 21st. A student of the history of the book and typography with a futurist streak, she now utilizes digital technology to bring fresh excitement to her letterpress printed artists' books and prints. Her collaborations with visual and performing artists, writers and philosophers result in structures that explore the book as performance art. Rice has taught and lectured extensively and is currently the manager of the digital arts and new media program at UCSC.

Work from the Press has been included in countless national and international exhibitions and collections, and has been honored by numerous awards and grants over the last 34 years.

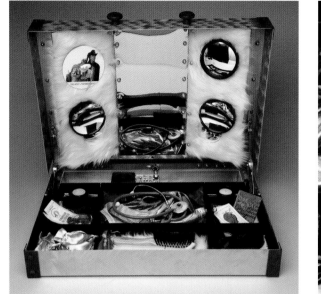

Documentado/ Undocumented. (work-in-progress)

Following page:
El alfabeto animado / The Lively Alphabet / Uywakunawan Qelqasqa

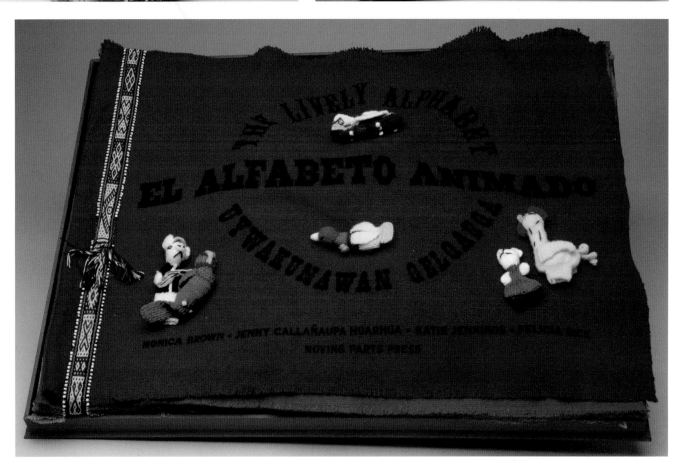

THE LIVELY ALPHABET

EL ALFABETO ANIMADO

QELQAKUNAWAN QELQASQA

MONICA BROWN • JENNY CALLAÑAUPA HUARHUA • KATIE JENNINGS • FELICIA RICE
MOVING PARTS PRESS

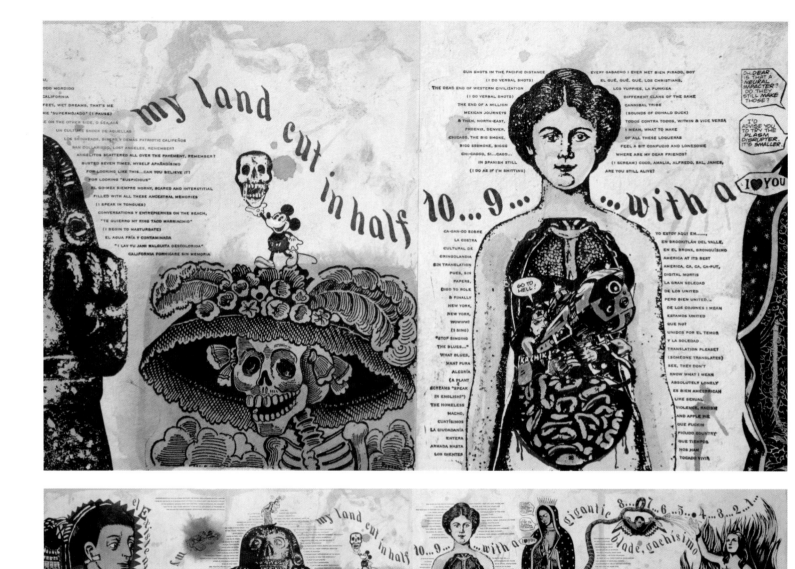

Codex Espangliensis: from Columbus to the Border Patrol

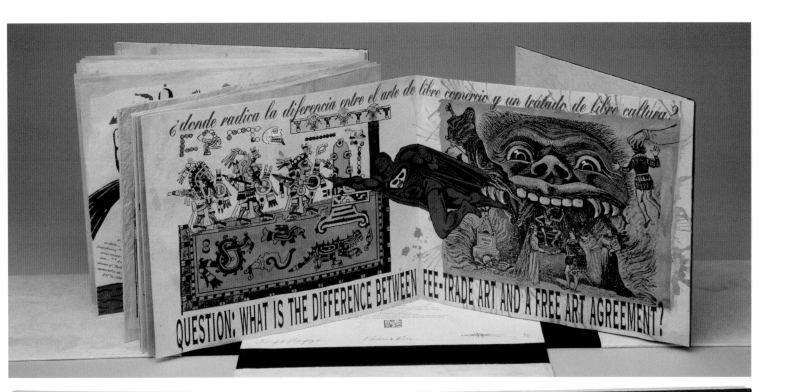

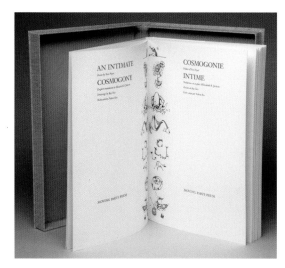
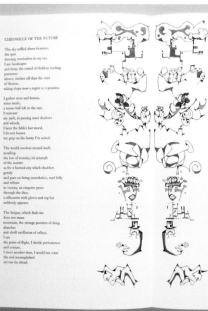
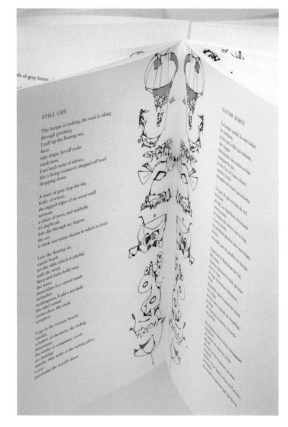

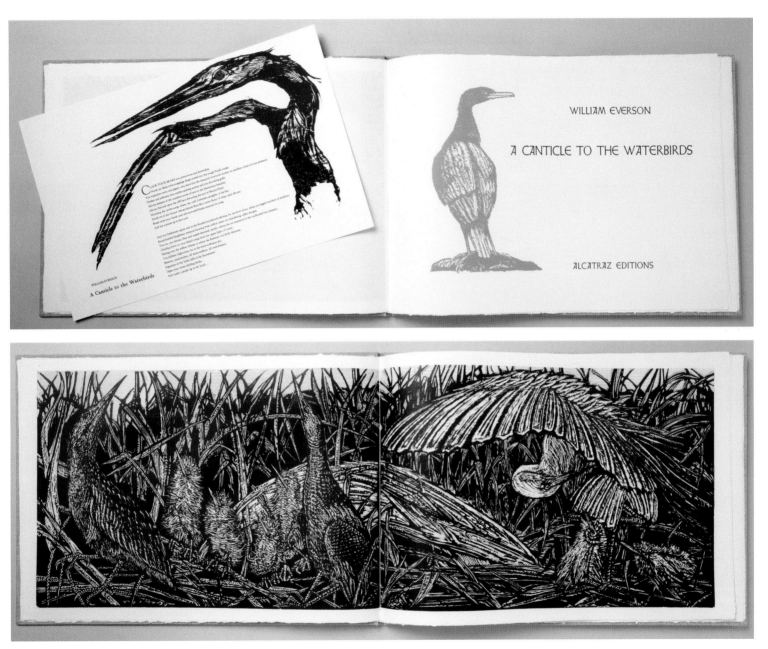

Previous page:
Cosmogonie Intime / An Intimate Cosmogony

A Canticle to the Waterbirds

WEYGANDT

PRINTS

MOVING PARTS PRESS

DAVID SWANGER

Kettle

A flat utensil against its horizon
as if wanting the invisible forearm

of some god to descend and brush
the brooding, secular world off its

sullen assumptions. Did Keats' urn
get it wrong? The beauty of truth

less than a chalice of light? Where's
love in a dark place? We run fingers

across the edges of others, experiments
which are not pointless. Need is not

pointless, even when it breeds dreams
like this one, a kettle without a smile,

a hard look at what sits on the shelf, alone.

Weygandt / Prints

Ninja Press

CAROLEE CAMPBELL
Sherman Oaks

Carolee Campbell inaugurated Ninja Press in 1984 in Sherman Oaks, California. Her interest in bookwork emerged from extensive experience as a photographer working in 19th- and 20th-century hand-coated processes. Turning photographic sequences into bound books led to bookbinding and eventually into printing with contemporary poetry at its heart. Campbell designs, prints, and binds each edition of books, which frequently include her photographs and artwork.

Campbell's artistic training began at age fifteen in the theatre in Los Angeles. At twenty she moved to New York City to study and work as an actor. Her substantial training at The Actors Studio under Lee Strasberg laid the groundwork for a sensibility she would later employ at Ninja Press—a well mediated balance between the rational (processes and techniques) and the irrational (intuition).

In 1976, after starring for nine years in the television show, "The Doctors," and winning an Emmy for her leading role in an NBC dramatic special, Campbell took her leave from acting.

In 2010 the 25th anniversary of the press was celebrated with a retrospective exhibition at Lafayette College in Easton, Pennsylvania. The entire Ninja Press archive is held in the Davidson Library Special Collections Department at the University of California, Santa Barbara.

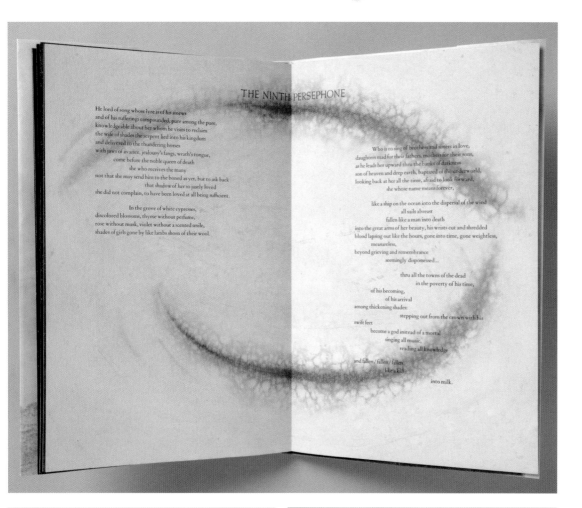

THE NINTH PERSEPHONE

He lord of song whose lyre is of his sinews
and of his sufferings compounded, pure among the pure,
knowledgeable about her whom he visits to reclaim
the wife of shades the serpent lied into his kingdom
and delivered to the thundering horses
with jaws of avarice, jealousy's fangs, wrath's tongue,
        come before the noble queen of death
            she who receives the many
not that she may send him to the boned as yet, but to ask back
            that shadow of her so justly loved
she did not complain, to have been loved at all being sufficient.

        In the grove of white cypresses,
discolored blossoms, thyme without perfume,
rose without musk, violet without a scented smile,
shades of girls gone by like lambs shorn of their wool.

                    Who is to sing of brothers and sisters in love,
            daughters mad for their fathers, mothers for their sons,
        as he leads her upward thru the banks of darkness
        son of heaven and deep earth, baptized of the underworld,
        looking back at her all the time, afraid to look forward,
                she whose name means forever,

            like a ship on the ocean into the dispersal of the wind
                all sails abreast
                    fallen like a man into death
        into the great arms of her beauty, his wrists cut and shredded
        blood lapsing out like the hours, gone into time, gone weightless,
                measureless,
        beyond grieving and remembrance
                seemingly dispossessed...

                    thru all the towns of the dead
                            in the poverty of his time,
            of his becoming,
                of his arrival
        among thickening shades:
                        stepping out from the crown with his
        swift feet
            become a god instead of a mortal
                singing all music,
                    reading all knowledge
    and fallen / fallen / fallen
                like a kid

                            into milk.

The Persephones.

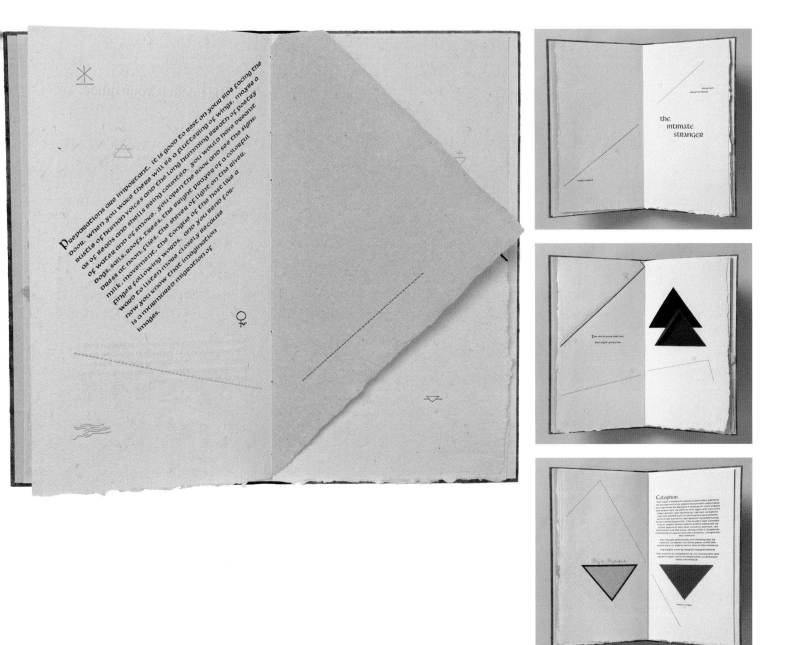

Preparations are important. It is good to rest on your side facing the door. When you wake there will be a fluttering of wings, maybe a rustle of human voices and the long humming breath of poetry as of water and of smoke. You open the book and see the signs: dogs, sails, roofs, trees, the night prayer of a colorful dress at noon, flies, the shiver of light on the river, milk, movement, the tongue of the host like a finger following woods, and you bend forward to listen more closely because now you know that imagination is a murmured migration of images.

The Intimate Stranger

MICHAEL HANNON

BURN DOWN THE ZENDO

What is Mind?

A wind-smeared mountain lake,
the least substantial of clouds,
giant waves breaking in the moonlight.

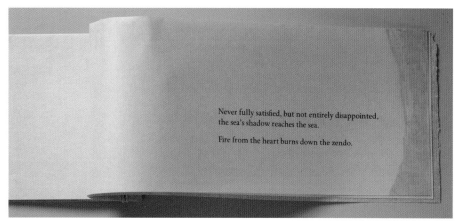

Never fully satisfied, but not entirely disappointed,
the sea's shadow reaches the sea.

Fire from the heart burns down the zendo.

Burn Down the Zendo

XIV

the ocean is there, always
just out of sight, out of
reach, its smell enveloping
us like a second skin

XXIV Short Love Poems

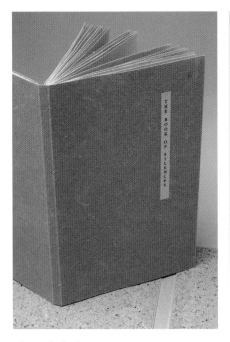

The Book of Silences

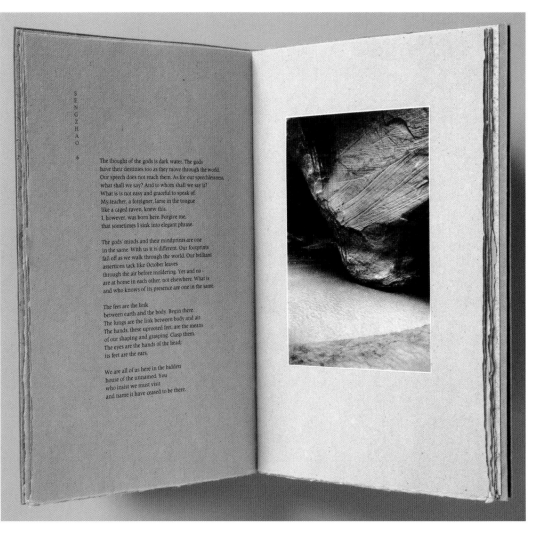

SENGZHAO 6

The thought of the gods is dark water. The gods
have their destinies too as they move through the world.
Our speech does not reach them. As for our speechlessness,
what shall we say? And to whom shall we say it?
What is is not easy and graceful to speak of.
My teacher, a foreigner, lame in the tongue
like a caged raven, knew this.
I, however, was born here. Forgive me,
that sometimes I sink into elegant phrase.

The gods' minds and their mindprints are one
in the same. With us it is different. Our footprints
fall off as we walk through the world. Our brilliant
assertions tack like October leaves
through the air before moldering. Yes and no -
are at home in each other, not elsewhere. What is
and who knows of its presence are one in the same.

The feet are the link
between earth and the body. Begin there.
The lungs are the link between body and air.
The hands, these uprooted feet, are the means
of our shaping and grasping. Clasp them.
The eyes are the hands of the head;
its feet are the ears.

We are all of us here in the hidden
house of the unnamed. You
who insist we must visit
and name it have ceased to be there.

ARCHI
TEXT
URES
THE
1-7
NATHANIEL TARN

The Architextures 1-7: "The Man of Music"

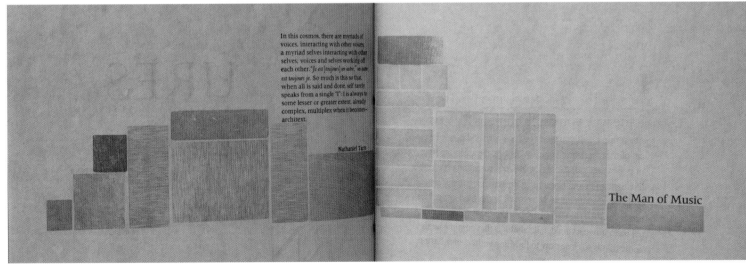

In this cosmos, there are myriads of voices, interacting with other voices, a myriad selves interacting with other selves, voices and selves working off each other. *"Je est [toujours] un autre," un autre est toujours je.* So much is this so that, when all is said and done, self rarely speaks from a single "I": it is always to some lesser or greater extent, already complex, multiplex when it becomes architext.

Nathaniel Tarn

The Man of Music

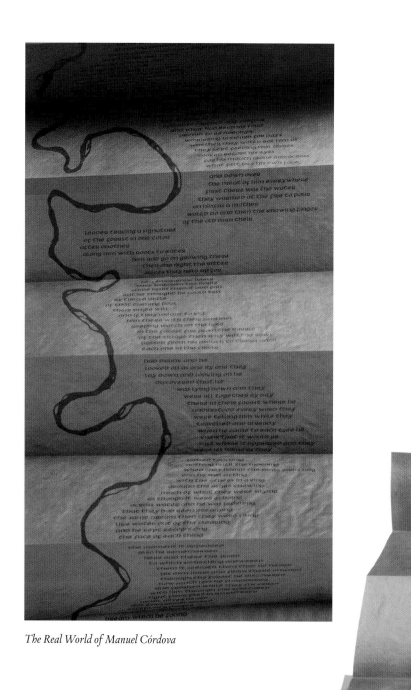

The Real World of Manuel Córdova

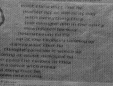

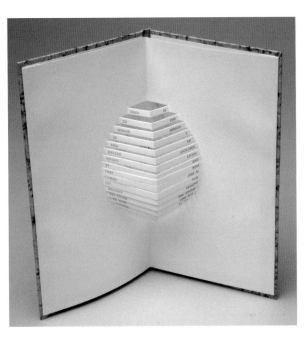

Mirror

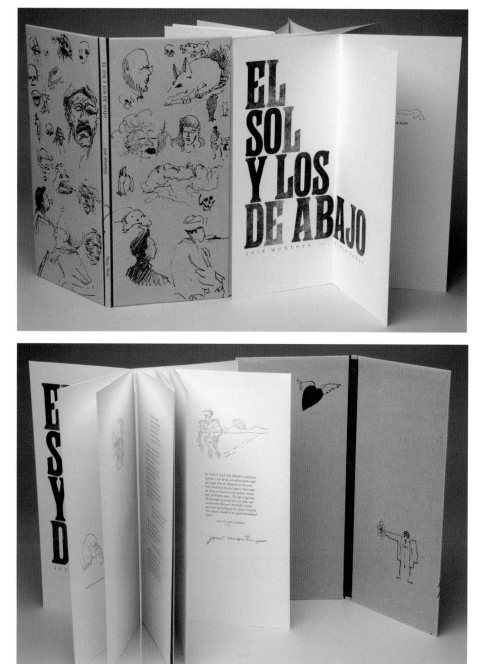

El Sol y Los de Abajo

Peter Koch Printer

PETER RUTLEDGE KOCH
Berkeley

Peter Rutledge Koch started printing in Missoula, Montana, when he founded Black Stone Press and *Montana Gothic: A Journal of Poetry, Literature & Graphics*. The press, established to publish the works of Koch's friends and colleagues, soon grew to include his first wife and partner, Shelley Hoyt. After four years of maverick literary production and self-instruction in typographic design, Koch moved the press to San Francisco.

After the dissolution of Black Stone Press in 1983 Koch struck out on his own to publish under numerous imprints, creatively named to suit different facets of his work: Peter Koch, Printers; Hormone Derange Editions; and Editions Koch. Today, the Koch studio in Berkeley is filled with ever increasing collections of books, prints, paintings, rare typefaces, antique printing equipment, and a generous assortment of printers, associates, apprentices, and friends.

The work of the press has grown over the years to include a deep commitment to publishing ancient Greek philosophers and Koch's personal vision of the Western landscape extracted from historic documents and photographic archives.

In 2005 Koch and his wife Susan Filter founded the CODEX Foundation and book fair to foster and preserve the arts of the printed book in the 21st Century.

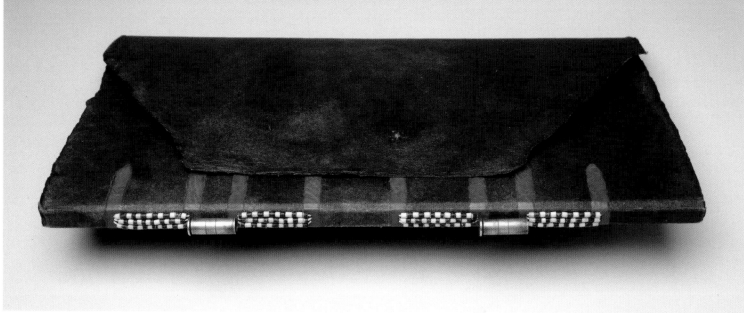

The Lost Journals of Sacajewea.

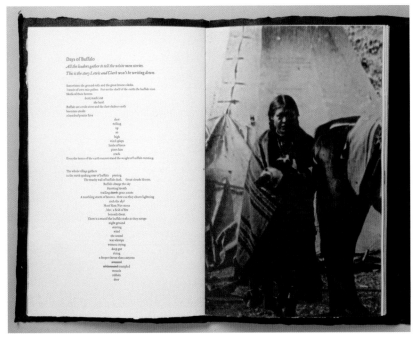

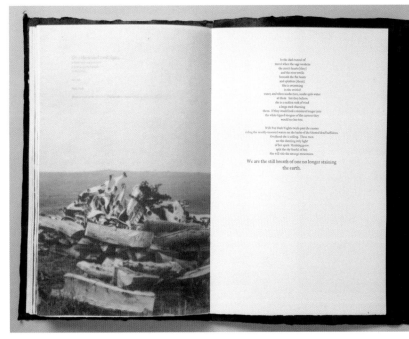

Building Mandan Camp

There is no fever
like the fever of white men building
the sound of trees falling
hissing
the branches of bones snapping/cracking/dying.

Building
they are building their houses.

One day their buildings will devour the sky.

Wood dies slowly.
Floorboards moan.
                    Walls shift
                                split light
I wake to the sound of trees praying
their glittering sap mourning
trees gathered shoulder to shoulder
shuddering
loss.

Wind gusts over
the spirit-glazed river
shrieks
webs of cracks.
The ghost of the river is creaking.

In early morning darkness
the white men hunt
all day
come back
with only
a single squirrel
rabbits twitching in the palms of their hands
mean in their hunger.

Silver birds spear dawns lonesome as song.
Cracked ice glitters violet.
Sun rises.   Sky sears white

JUST BEFORE SUN SLEEPS
SKY TURNS SHADES OF WILD ROSES.

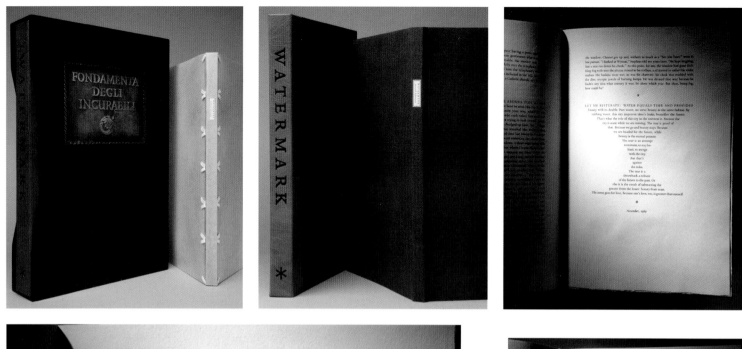

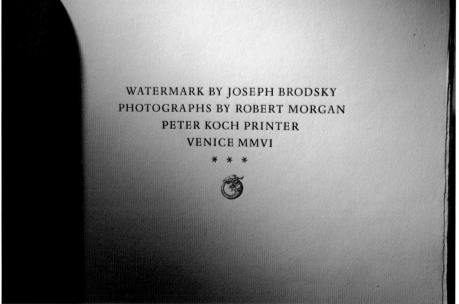

WATERMARK BY JOSEPH BRODSKY
PHOTOGRAPHS BY ROBERT MORGAN
PETER KOCH PRINTER
VENICE MMVI

* * *

Watermark

vast herds of Buffaloe deer Elk and Antelopes more seen feeding in every direction as far as the eye of the observer could reach.

CROWBAIT

Nature Morte

The Fragments of PARMENIDES & an English translation by ROBERT BRINGHURST

Wood engravings by RICHARD WAGENER

EDITIONS KOCH, Berkeley, 2003

The Fragments of Parmenides

Zebra Noise
with a flatted seventh

Finished print and
engraved wood block for
W: Cotton boll weevil,
Anthonomus grandis

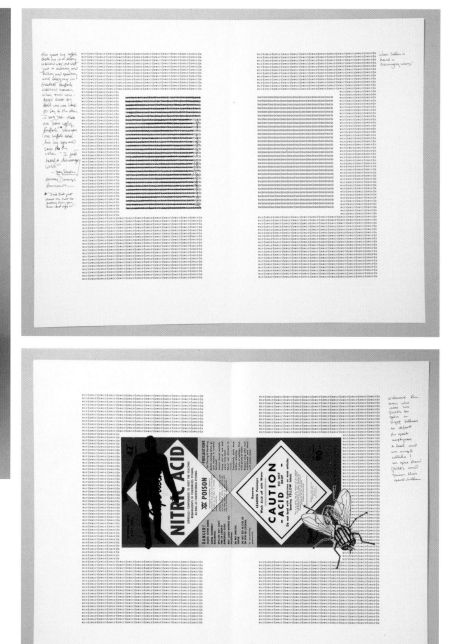

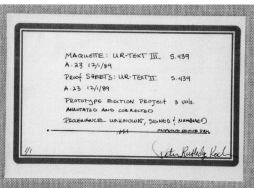

MAQUETTE: UR-TEXT III   S.439
A.23 12/1/89
PROOF SHEETS: UR-TEXT II   S.439
A.23 12/1/89
PROTOTYPE EDITION PROJECT 3 vols.
ANNOTATED AND CORRECTED
PROVENANCE UNKNOWN, SIGNED & NUMBERED
————— ENDGRAIN EDITOR DR4
1/1   *Peter Rutledge Koch*

upper left & lower right:
Ur-Text Volume 1

Above & left:
Ur-Text Volume 2

Upper right:
Ur-Text Volume 3

A RICH MAN TOOK
DIOGENES INTO HIS
HOUSE AND WARNED
HIM NOT TO SPIT ON
THE EXPENSIVE RUGS OR
FURNISHINGS, WHERE-
UPON HE SPAT IN THE
MAN'S FACE, SAYING THAT
HE COULD FIND NOTHING
ELSE THERE CHEAP
ENOUGH TO SPIT ON.

HE WOULD MAKE THE
ROUNDS OF THE ORNA
MENTED PORTICOS OF
ATHENS, BEGGING ALMS
FROM THE PUBLIC STATUES

Diogenes: Defictions

DIOGENES SAT IN THE
PUBLIC SQUARE ONE
AFTERNOON GLUEING
SHUT THE PAGES OF
A BOOK.

D WALK
ARD T

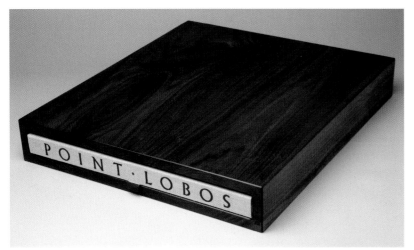

Point Lobos

POINT LOBOS

A PORTFOLIO OF FIFTEEN POEMS BY
ROBINSON JEFFERS & FIFTEEN PHOTO-
GRAPHS BY WOLF VON DEM BUSSCHE
INTRODUCED BY WILLIAM EVERSON
& PRINTED BY PETER RUTLEDGE KOCH
FOR PETER AND THE WOLF EDITIONS
OAKLAND, CALIFORNIA MCMLXXXVII

Turkey Press

HARRY REESE & SANDRA LIDDELL REESE
Isla Vista

Harry Reese founded Turkey Press in 1974 while he was a graduate student at Brown University. He moved to Berkeley, California a year later, where he met Sandra Liddell Paulson, who was, by day, teaching in the San Francisco School District and, by night, serving cocktails at the St. Francis Hotel. In 1977 the couple moved from Berkeley to Isla Vista, where they married and became equal partners in Turkey Press.

For more than three decades Harry and Sandra Reese have centered their work on the imaginative possibilities of the book as a container of thought, visual space, and beauty. Their early publications consisted primarily of small volumes of letterpress printed poetry, distinguished by the use of their own handmade paper and relief printmaking. In addition to editing and designing their books, the Reeses hand set type, print, bind, make paper, and produce most of the visual art for their editions entirely in house. In 1990, they began collaborating with other visual artists and writers to create limited edition artist books under the imprint Edition Reese.

Harry Reese is a professor in the Department of Art and Associate Dean of the College of Creative Studies, where he directs the Book Arts Program, at the University of California, Santa Barbara. Sandra Reese devotes her full attention to printing and binding their publications. The Getty Research Institute acquired the Turkey Press archives in 1992.

33 1/3: Off the Record

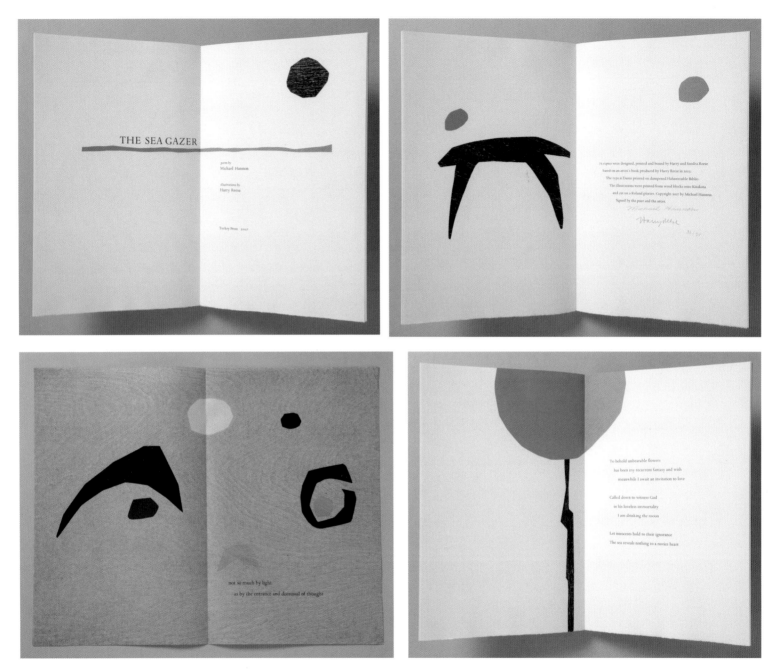

The Sea Gazer

Following page: *Kinnikinnick Brand Kickapoo Joy-Juice*

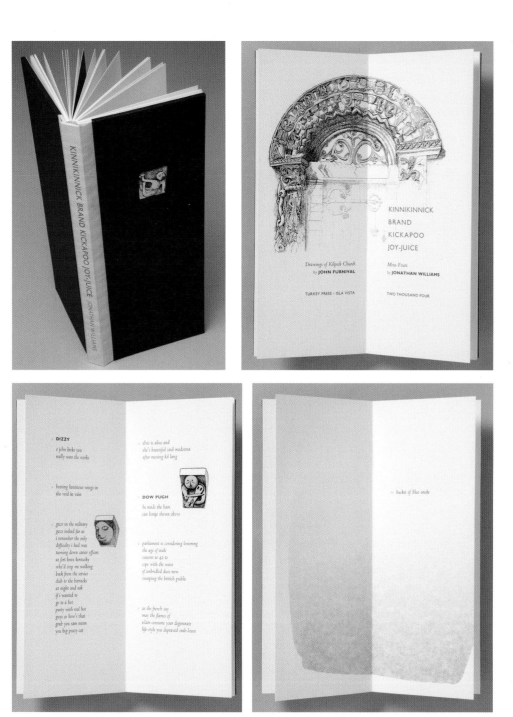

27   we all start plucking
      turkeys this next tuesday

28   ian gardner used to
      make two bob an
      hour separating copulating monkeys
      with a long stick
      sunday afternoons in the
      local zoo at heysham
      in lancashire families insisted
      no sex please we're
      british you filthy beasts

29   this morning henry pulled
      down the morning-glory vines
      from the pony stable

Things are done
Sudden jolt.
Fear Alarm.

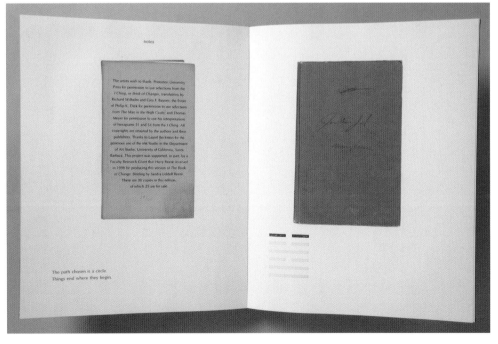

The path chosen is a circle.
Things end where they begin.

Grasshopper

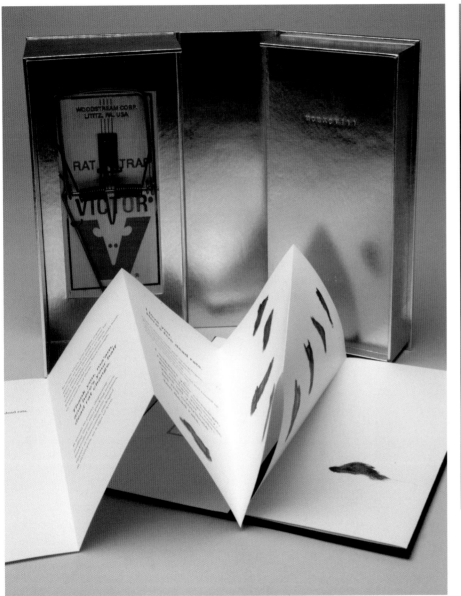

**I love you.
Here's five dead rats.**

Gold is fine in teeth and on ring fingers.
Rats would liberate the ghettos,
turn the economy belly-up.
Even the commonest man could pull himself up
by his own smelly bootstraps.

**I support your campaign,
respect your humanity,
get contact high cosmic
vibes off your smile:
let me contribute
ten dead rats.**

The Standard

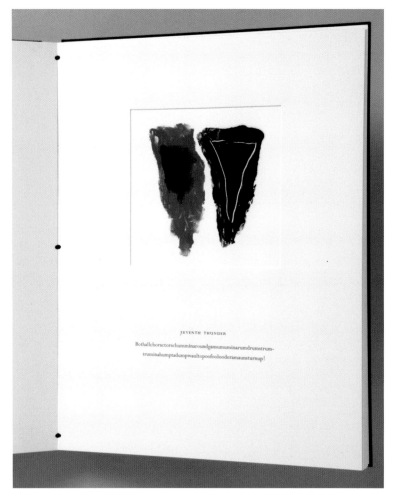

SEVENTH THUNDER

Bothallchoractorschumminaroundgansumuminarumdrumstrum-
truminahumptadumpwaultopoofoolooderamaunsturnup!

Funagainstawake

(Bababadalgharaghtakamminarronnkonnbronntonne
rronntuonnthunntrovarrhounawnskawntoohoohoordenen
thurnuk!)(Perkodhuskurunbarggruauyagokgorlayorgrom
gremmitghundhurthrumathunaradidillifaititillibumul
lunukkunun!)(Klikkaklakkaklaskaklopatzklatschabatta
creppycrottygraddaghsemmihsammihnouithappluddyap
pladdypkonpkot!)Bladyughfoulmoecklenburgwhurawhoras
cortastrumpapornanennykocksapastippatappatupperstrip
puckputtanach,eh?Thingcrooklyexineverypasturesixdix
likencehimaroundhersthemaggerbykinkinkankanwithdown
mindlookingated**funaginstawake**Lukkedoerenduna
ndurraskewdylooshoofermoyportertooryzooysphalnabor
tansporthaokansakroidverjkapakkapukBothallchorac
torschumminaroundgansumuminarumdrumstrumtruminah
umptadumpwaultopoofoolooderamaunsturnup!Pappappap
parrassannuaragheallachnatullaghmonganmacmacmacw
hackfalltherdebblenonthedubblandaddydoodled(Husstenhas
stencaffincoffintussemtossemdamandamnacosagheusaghh
obixhatouxpeswchbechoscashlcarcarcaract)Ullhodturden
weirmudgaardgringnirurdrmolnirfenrirlukkilokkibaugiman
dodrrerinsurtkrinmgernrackinarockar!Thor'sforyo!

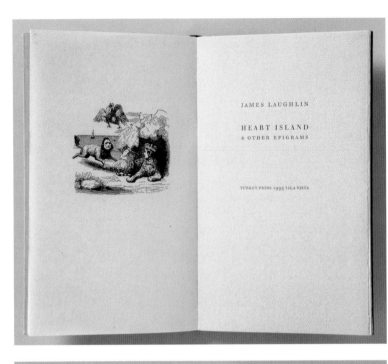

JAMES LAUGHLIN

HEART ISLAND
& OTHER EPIGRAMS

TURKEY PRESS 1995 ISLA VISTA

FOR THE FINDERS WITHIN

I cannot name them nor
tell from whence they

come   I cannot summon
them nor make them lin-

ger   they come when they
wish (and when least ex-

pected) and in a moment
they are gone leaving

their burst of words
which become my song.

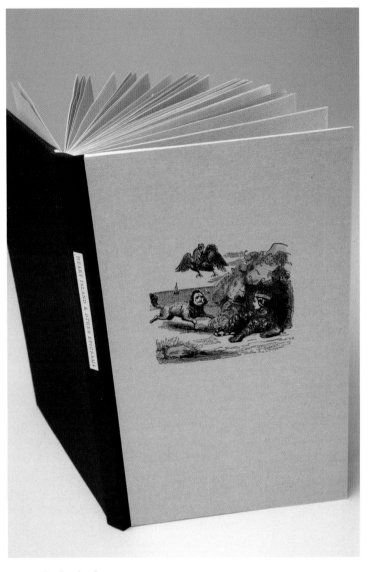

Heart Island and Other Epigrams

arplines

harry reese

an edition of 43 copies on arches cover
images, printing & cover painting by harry reese
chemise & box binding by sandra liddell reese
text adapted from a 1980 turkey press book
inspired by lines of jean (hans) arp

23/43

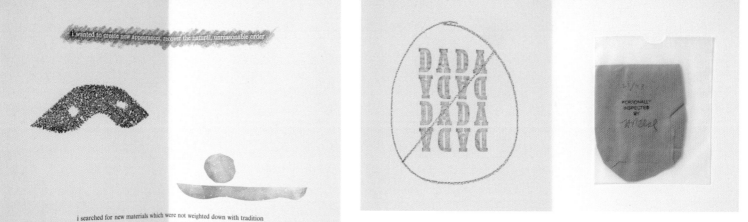

i wanted to create new appearances, recover the natural, unreasonable order

i searched for new materials which were not weighted down with tradition

Arplines

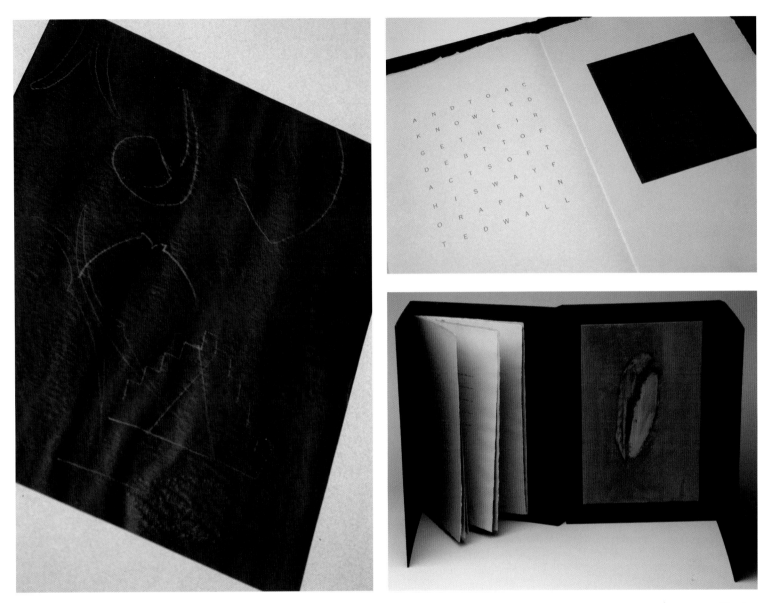

Turnings

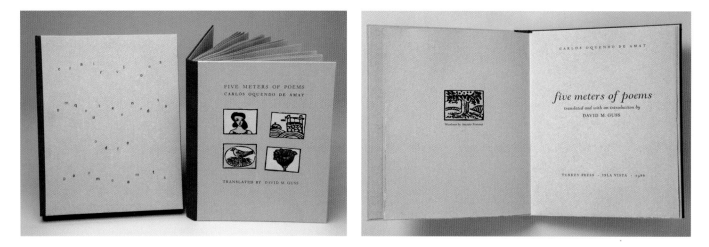

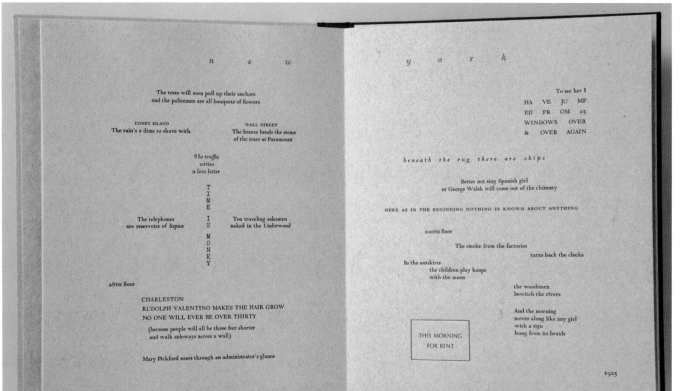

*Five Meters
of Poems*

A Chronology of Fine Printing in California

ROBERT BRINGHURST

1798   Agustín Juan Vicente Zamorano born at San Agustín, Florida (which was then a Spanish possession).

1832   Édouard (later Edward) Bosqui born in Montréal.

1834   Zamorano, now an agent of the Spanish crown, acquires some worn type and a used wood-frame press, probably built by Adam Ramage in Philadelphia. The press and type, having just been shipped from Boston to Honolulu, are shipped again from Honolulu to Monterey, where Zamorano produces the first books, pamphlets and broadsides printed in California.

1842   Zamorano dies in San Diego.

1863   Bosqui establishes his first engraving and printing office in San Francisco.

1866   Andrew Foreman, a Scottish typefounder, moves to San Francisco, establishes a foundry, and casts the first type made in California.

1871   John Henry Nash born in Woodbridge, Ontario. (Woodbridge has since been absorbed into Vaughan, which has in its turn become a suburb of Toronto.)

——   Edward DeWitt Taylor born in San Francisco.

——   Porter Garnett born in San Francisco.

c.1873   Simons & Co., San Francisco, begins to manufacture the California job case.

1874   Nelson Crocker Hawks moves to San Francisco and establishes the Pacific Type Foundry (a branch of the Marder, Luse Foundry, Chicago).

——   John Julius Johnck born in Keokuk, Iowa.

1875   Ellis Read, an Australian working in San Francisco, becomes the West Coast agent for the Miller & Richard typefoundry, Edinburgh.

1877   Nelson Hawks, in San Francisco, devises the American point system with 12 points to the pica and 6 picas to the inch. (This will be revised at a meeting in Chicago in 1886 so that one pica is precisely 0.166 inch and 6 picas = 0.996 inch). By the end of the 19th century, this system of typographic measurement will be in daily use throughout the English-speaking world.

——   Edward Bosqui and the lithographer William Harring, in San Francisco, produce the first book printed in California by chromolithography.

1879   Henry Huntly Taylor, Edward's younger brother, born in San Francisco.

1881   Bruce McCallister born in Madison, South Dakota.

1884   "The Loan Book Exhibition," UC Berkeley, displays 470 items, ranging from manuscripts and incunabula to recent printing and binding, drawn from Bay Area public libraries and private collections.

1887   In Washington, D.C., Tolbert Lanston, a lawyer by profession, builds his first keyboard-operated typesetting machine and christens it the Monotype. As initially designed, the machine forms type, one letter at a time, from cold metal blanks. It is not a success.

——   John Henry Nash apprentices with the printer James Murray in Toronto.

1889   Edwin Grabhorn born in Cincinnati.

1891   Carroll Timanus Harris born in Harper's Ferry, West Virginia.

1892   Pacific Type Foundry, San Francisco, becomes a branch of the new ATF (American Type Founders) conglomerate.

1895   John Henry Nash moves to San Francisco and finds work with the Hicks-Judd printing company.

1896 Edward Taylor opens his first printing firm, E.D. Taylor Co., in San Francisco.

— Tolbert Lanston redesigns his Monotype machine so that it casts from hot metal, and the Lanston Monotype Co. issues its first original typeface. Still, the machine has few supporters.

1898 E.D. Taylor Co. ceases operation and is replaced by Stanley-Taylor, a partnership of Edward Taylor and D.S. Stanley. John Henry Nash is employed by this firm intermittently from its inception to 1903.

1899 In Philadelphia, John Sellers Bancroft redesigns and improves Lanston's Monotype machine. Two separate manufacturing and marketing facilities are then initiated by two independent companies: one based in Philadelphia, the other near Redhill, south of London.

1900 Robert Grabhorn, Edwin's younger brother, born in Indianapolis.

— Wilder Bentley born in San Francisco.

— Lawton Kennedy born in San Francisco.

1902 Grant Dahlstrom born in Idaho Falls.

— Ansel Adams born in San Francisco.

1903 Nash and his fellow Canadian Bruce Brough found the Twentieth Century Press in San Francisco. This is quickly absorbed into Paul Elder's Tomoyé Press, with Nash in charge of typography and design.

1905 Yisroel Chaim Miodownik (later Saul Marks) born in Warsaw.

— Ward Ritchie born in Los Angeles.

— Bancroft Library founded at UC Berkeley.

1906 Bruce McCallister arrives in San Francisco on the day of the great earthquake and heads promptly for Los Angeles.

1908 Lewis Allen born in San Francisco.

— Dorothy Caswell (later Dorothy Allen) born in Linton, Indiana.

— Gregg Anderson born. After the early death of their parents, he and his younger brother will be raised by an aunt, Edith Sinclair, in Pasadena.

1909 Lillian Simon (later Lillian Marks) born in Ozorków, northwest of Łódź.

1910 Daniel Berkeley Updike, proprietor of the Merrymount Press in Boston, begins teaching typographic history at Harvard University's recently founded Graduate School of Business – a task he will continue through 1917. It is the first such course ever offered in a university setting.

1911 Nash leaves Tomoyé Press and, with Edward and Henry Taylor, forms the partnership Taylor, Nash, & Taylor. Stanley-Taylor is dissolved and its assets are absorbed by the new partnership. Henry Taylor soon takes leave of absence to study with Updike at Harvard.

— Martha Jane Bissell (later Jane Grabhorn) born in San Francisco.

1912 Book Club of California founded in San Francisco.

— William Everson born in Sacramento.

1913 Lillian Simon moves with her family to Detroit.

1914 Henry Taylor completes his course of study with Updike in typographic history and returns to San Francisco with his Harvard MBA.

1915 Partnership of Taylor, Nash, & Taylor dissolved; Edward and Henry Taylor continue as Taylor & Taylor, San Francisco.

— George Mackenzie spends the year in San Francisco demonstrating Monotype keyboarding and casting at the Panama Pacific Exposition, then remains in the city and founds the Monotype Composition Co.

— Edwin Grabhorn establishes his Studio Press in Indianapolis.

1916 Nash opens his own composing room in San Francisco.

1917 Edward Bosqui dies in San Francisco.

1918	Yisroel Miodownik begins his printing apprenticeship in Warsaw.
1919	Edwin and Robert Grabhorn move to San Francisco.
—	Carroll Harris moves to San Francisco as assistant regional manager for Lanston Monotype; he stays for two years.
—	Huntington Library established in San Marino.
1920	Jack Werner Stauffacher born in San Francisco. He will move at age two with his family to San Mateo, and will teach himself to print at age 14.
—	In Philadelphia, Frederic Goudy is appointed artistic director for the Lanston Monotype Company – a position he will hold until his death in 1947. During the next quarter century, many of the faces he designs – some for Lanston Monotype and others for handsetting – will find their way to California.
1921	John Johnck arrives in San Francisco. With Wallace Kibbee, he soon forms the printing firm of Johnck, Kibbee & Co.
—	Porter Garnett moves to Pittsburgh to teach at Carnegie Tech.
—	Yisroel Miodownik moves from Poland to the USA and takes the name Saul Marks.
—	Both the American and the English Monotype operations issue their first historical revival typeface. The American face is called Garamont, the English one Garamond, and both are sold as French Renaissance types (though both are in fact based on the French Baroque designs of Jean Jannon) – and both soon find their way to California.
1922	In England, Stanley Morison is appointed typographical advisor to the Monotype Corporation. Over the next twenty years, English Monotype will produce, at Morison's urging, matrices for casting many new printing types and historical revivals. A number of these will find their way to California.

1923	Carroll Harris returns to San Francisco and arranges to join George Mackenzie's Monotype Composition Co.
—	Garnett establishes the Laboratory Press in Pittsburgh.
—	Adrian Wilson born in Ann Arbor, Michigan.
1926	The Monotype Composition Co. of San Francisco is reborn as Mackenzie & Harris.
—	Valenti Angelo begins illustrating books for the Grabhorn Press.
—	Grant Dahlstrom begins a year of study with Porter Garnett and the Laboratory Press, Philadelphia.
1927	Partnership of Johnck & Kibbee dissolved. Harold Seeger joins Johnck in the firm Johnck & Seeger.
—	Grant Dahlstrom moves to Los Angeles and begins to work as a typographer and book designer in association with Bruce McCallister.
—	Gregg Anderson starts work at the Huntington Library and establishes the Grey Bow Press in Pasadena with Roland Baughman.
—	Ansel Adams assembles his first photographic portfolio.
—	Roxburghe Club of San Francisco founded.
—	Zamorano Club founded in Los Angeles.
—	Saul Marks and Lillian Simon married in Detroit.
—	Bruce Rogers's Centaur type (first cut in 1914) is adapted for the Monotype machine. With Frederic Warde's Arrighi, adapted for the Monotype in 1929, it will become a favorite face at Mackenzie & Harris, used by many of California's finest printers.
1930	Anderson starts work at the Grabhorn Press, San Francisco, and the Grey Bow Press ceases operation.
1930	Ward Ritchie leaves for a year in Paris, much of it spent working in the studio of François-Louis Schmied.
—	Saul and Lillian Marks move to Los Angeles where, in the following year, they found the Plantin Press.
1931	Wilder Bentley begins three years of study with Porter Garnett at the Laboratory Press.

— James Elliott joins Taylor & Taylor.

— Rounce & Coffin Club founded in Los Angeles.

1932 Ward Ritchie founds Ward Ritchie Press, in a barn behind his parents' house in Los Angeles.

— Lewis Allen and Dorothy Caswell are married and begin printing together in San Francisco.

— Robert Grabhorn and Jane Bissell are married in San Francisco.

— Anderson starts work with Harold Hugo at Meriden Gravure in Meriden, Connecticut.

— Over the summer, Wilder Bentley delivers "History and Aesthetics of Fine Printing," a series of 12 public lectures at UC Berkeley.

1934 William Andrews Clark Library founded in Los Angeles.

1935 Porter Garnett closes the Laboratory Press, retires from Carnegie Tech, and returns to California, settling in Calistoga.

— Anderson returns to California and joins the Ward Ritchie Press.

— Wilder and Ellen Bentley establish the Archetype Press in Berkeley.

— Andrew Hoyem born in Sioux Falls, South Dakota.

— James Robertson born in Los Angeles.

1936 Carolee Campbell born in Los Angeles.

— John Johnck dies in San Francisco.

1937 Jack Stauffacher begins to visit Nash, the Grabhorns, Taylor & Taylor, and other San Francisco printers.

— Henry Taylor dies in San Francisco.

— Frederic Goudy is commissioned to design a typeface for the University of California Press. The type, University of California Old Style (later known simply as Californian), is completed early in 1938 and the type first used by UC Press in 1940.

— Anderson & Baughman's Grey Bow Press briefly revived.

1938 Nash leaves California, where commissions have dried up, and starts to teach at the University of Oregon.

— Sandra DeNola (later Kirshenbaum) born in Rome.

1939 Lewis and Dorothy Allen establish the Allen Press in San Francisco.

1940 The partnership of Anderson & Ritchie is formed alongside the Ward Ritchie Press.

1941 In San Mateo, Jack Stauffacher begins publishing books under the Greenwood Press imprint; he is drafted soon afterward and spends two years in Kentucky and Texas making military maps.

— Sandra DeNola (later Kirshenbaum), age three, arrives with her mother in San Francisco.

— Carolyn Sollis (later Carolyn Robertson) born in Salt Lake City.

1942 Gregg Anderson enters military service.

1943 Dahlstrom acquires control of the Castle Press, Pasadena.

— Peter Rutledge Koch born in Missoula, Montana.

— Wilder Bentley's Archetype Press suspends operation.

— John Henry Nash returns to California, settling in Berkeley.

— William Everson sent to Camp Angel, a work camp for conscientious objectors at Waldport, Oregon. There he refines his pressmanship under the tutelage of Joe Kalal, becomes "chairman of the committee on fine arts," and prints books written by himself and others.

1944 Gregg Anderson killed in Normandy.

— George Mackenzie dies in San Francisco.

— Adrian Wilson, a conscientious objector, arrives at Camp Angel and, working with Everson, gets his first taste of printing.

— Jack Stauffacher, discharged from the army, returns to San Mateo.

— Lawrence G. Van Velzer born in Los Angeles.

1945	The Allen Press relocates to Hillsborough (near San Mateo).	1951	The Allens leave for a year in Europe, printing a chapbook in Florence and a book in Cagnes-sur-Mer (just west of Nice).
——	Sumner Stone born in Venice, Florida.		
——	Bruce McCallister dies in Los Angeles.	——	Everson enters the Dominican order as Brother Antoninus and moves his press to St Albert's College, Oakland, renaming it the Albertus Magnus Press.
1946	Edward Taylor retires from Taylor & Taylor, and James Elliott assumes control of the firm.		
——	Everson returns to California from Waldport. He learns the rudiments of handpress operation from Wilder Bentley and James Hart in Berkeley, then buys a large handpress of his own and sets it up at Treesbank Farm near Sebastopol.	——	Porter Garnett dies in Calistoga.
		1952	The Allen Press relocates to Kentfield (near San Rafael).
		1954	Ward Ritchie begins designing books for the University of California Press.
——	Wilson arrives in San Francisco, begins printing on his own, and pays frequent visits to the Grabhorns and other fine printers in the area.	——	Felicia Rice born in San Francisco.
		1955	Stauffacher closes the Greenwood Press and leaves for three years' study in Italy, based in Florence.
——	Harry Eugene Reese born in Fort Worth, Texas.	1956	Peggy Gotthold born in Redwood City.
——	Andrew Hoyem, age 10, moves to China Lake, California with his parents.	——	Robert Slimbach born in Evanston, Illinois, and within a few years moves with his family to Southern California.
1947	Stauffacher moves Greenwood Press to San Francisco.		
——	Everson moves to Berkeley with his handpress and establishes the Equinox Press.	1957	The Allens leave for a second year in France, most of it spent printing in Antibes (between Cagnes and Cannes).
——	Sandra Liddell Paulson (later Sandra Liddell Reese) born in San Rafael.		
		1958	Adrian Wilson leaves for a year in the Netherlands, Germany, and England, where he works with John Dreyfus, John Peters, Will Carter, and David Kindersley.
——	John Henry Nash dies in Berkeley.		
1948	Wilson and Stauffacher form a short-lived printing partnership.		
1949	The exhibit *The French Art of the Book,* arranged by Carroll Harris, opens in San Francisco and breaks records for attendance.	——	Stauffacher returns to San Francisco from Florence, then moves at once to Pittsburgh, where he teaches for five years.
		——	Everson's Albertus Magnus Press ceases operation, and for the next 12 years he does no printing.
1950	Wilson begins designing for University of California Press.		
——	The Allen Press relocates to Belvedere, in Marin County, and becomes a full-time occupation for both proprietors.	——	Dave Haselwood, an aspiring poet from Kansas, founds the Auerhahn Press, San Francisco.
		1959	Carol Twombly born in Bedford, Massachusetts.
——	Everson moves his press to Maurin House, a Catholic Worker hostel in Oakland, and there renames it the Seraphim Press.	1960	Wilson opens a studio in Tuscany Alley, where he does more work as a free-lance designer of books than as a printer.

1961 Andrew Hoyem joins Dave Haselwood in the Auerhahn Press, San Francisco.

— Taylor & Taylor is dissolved.

— In Pittsburgh, Stauffacher founds the New Laboratory Press, reviving Porter Garnett's legacy, and works with Hermann Zapf.

1962 Edward DeWitt Taylor dies in San Francisco.

1963 Stauffacher closes the New Laboratory Press and moves to Palo Alto, becoming head of design at Stanford University Press.

1964 Lanston Monotype, Philadelphia, ceases to manufacture hot-metal typesetting machines and begins to import them from the UK.

1965 Grabhorn Press closes.

— Hoyem assumes full ownership of Auerhahn Press and changes the imprint to Andrew Hoyem, Printer.

1966 Robert Grabhorn and Andrew Hoyem enter into partnership as Grabhorn-Hoyem, which eventually acquires all surviving Grabhorn Press equipment.

— Stauffacher returns to San Francisco and reopens the Greenwood Press.

1967 Ansel Adams, Nancy Newhall, Adrian Wilson and others teach the first of four annual workshops entitled *Images and Words: The Making of a Photographic Book* at UC Santa Cruz.

1968 Edwin Grabhorn dies in San Francisco.

1969 Everson leaves the Dominicans and reverts to his secular name.

1971 Everson founds Lime Kiln Press at McHenry Library, UC Santa Cruz.

1973 Robert Grabhorn dies in San Francisco.

— Jane Grabhorn dies in San Francisco.

— Palo Alto Research Center produces a machine called the Alto – arguably the first desktop computer.

1974 Andrew Hoyem establishes Arion Press, successor to Grabhorn-Hoyem.

— Felicia Rice studies with Jack Stauffacher at the Cowell Press, UC Santa Cruz in a program that lapses after one year.

— James and Carolyn Robertson (who married in 1971) establish the Yolla Bolly Press as a design studio near Covelo, in Mendocino County.

— Saul Marks dies in Los Angeles; the Plantin Press continues under Lillian Marks.

— Peter Koch establishes Black Stone Press in Missoula.

— Harry Reese establishes Turkey Press in Cranston, Rhode Island.

1975 Carroll Harris dies in San Francisco.

— Sandra Kirshenbaum founds the quarterly journal *Fine Print* (later *Fine Print: A Review for the Arts of the Book*) in San Francisco.

— Ward Ritchie establishes Laguna Verde Imprenta in Laguna Verde.

— Felicia Rice works with Everson at the Lime Kiln Press, UC Santa Cruz.

— Harry Reese moves, with his Turkey Press imprint, to Berkeley.

1976 Apple Computer Co. established in Cupertino.

1977 Rice establishes Moving Parts Press in Santa Cruz.

— Sandra Liddell Reese joins Harry Reese as a partner in Turkey Press.

— The Allen Press makes the last of its many moves, from Kentfield to Greenbrae, two miles away.

1978 Peter Koch moves to San Francisco, reopens Black Stone Press in partnership with Shelley Hoyt-Koch, and begins a year-long apprenticeship at Tuscany Alley with Adrian Wilson.

— Harry Reese begins teaching at UC Santa Barbara; Turkey Press relocates to Isla Vista.

— Frances Butler, Kathy Walkup, Betsy Davids, and others found the Pacific Center for the Book Arts, San Francisco.

1979   The exhibition *Five Fine Printers: Jack Stauffacher, Adrian Wilson, Richard Bigus, Andrew Hoyem, William Everson* is mounted at UC Davis. Sandra Kirshenbaum compiles the catalogue.

—— Grant Dahlstrom sells the Castle Press and retires from printing.

1980   Felicia Rice works at Tuscany Alley with Adrian Wilson.

—— Charles Bigelow becomes typography editor of *Fine Print*.

—— Dahlstrom dies in Pasadena.

—— Lawton Kennedy dies in Berkeley.

1981   Rice inherits the shop and typographic library of Sherwood Grover, former pressman at the Grabhorn Press.

1982   Everson's Lime Kiln Press ceases operation.

—— Van Velzer begins to work at Arion Press in San Francisco, where he will continue for 12 years.

—— Adobe Systems, Inc., founded in Mountain View, California. Its core product is a so-called "page description language" called PostScript. The company is soon producing scalable digital versions of existing metal typefaces using this language. In doing so, it establishes the PostScript pica as precisely one sixth of an inch – as Nelson Hawks proposed in San Francisco in 1877.

1983   James and Carolyn Robertson shift the focus of Yolla Bolly Press to the production of letterpress limited editions.

—— Charles Bigelow becomes part-time typographic advisor to Adobe Systems.

1984   Carolee Campbell establishes Ninja Press in Sherman Oaks.

—— Peter Koch closes Black Stone Press and opens a studio in Oakland under the imprint Peter Koch, Printer.

—— Peggy Gotthold works with Felicia Rice at Moving Parts Press in Santa Cruz.

—— Sumner Stone becomes Director of Typography at Adobe Systems, Mountain View, and introduces several Bay Area letterpress printers to digital typography.

—— Ansel Adams dies in Monterey.

1985   Peggy Gotthold apprentices briefly at the Yolla Bolly Press in Covelo.

—— The Plantin Press is dissolved.

—— Carol Twombly begins working part-time at Adobe Systems in Mountain View.

1987   Robert Slimbach becomes Adobe Systems' first resident type designer, and Adobe begins producing original type designs.

—— Monotype Corporation (UK) ceases the manufacture of hot-metal typesetting machines.

1988   Adrian Wilson dies in San Francisco.

—— Peggy Gotthold begins to work at Arion Press in San Francisco, where she will continue for 12 years.

—— Carol Twombly joins Slimbach as a full-time type designer at Adobe Systems.

1989   Andrew Hoyem acquires Mackenzie & Harris's hot-metal division and renames the company M&H Type.

—— Sumner Stone leaves Adobe and soon establishes his own digital type foundry.

—— Wilder Bentley dies in Berkeley.

1990   Van Velzer and Gotthold establish Foolscap Press in Berkeley.

—— Peter Koch abandons his Oakland studio, wrecked by the Loma Prieta earthquake, and moves his presses to Berkeley.

—— The Reeses establish a second imprint, Edition Reese, in Isla Vista.

—— After 15 years, the journal *Fine Print* ceases publication (a final issue, the index, will follow in 2003).

	Around this date, fine letterpress printers begin to adopt photopolymer plates. These permit the conversion of digital type to three dimensions.
1991	Adobe Systems, Mountain View, acquires a license to produce digital versions of the entire Monotype library of typefaces.
	Lillian Marks dies in Los Angeles.
1992	Rice relocates her Moving Parts Press to Bonny Doon, northwest of Santa Cruz.
	The Allen Press in Greenbrae ceases operation.
1994	William Everson dies at Kingfisher Flat, near Santa Cruz.
1996	Ward Ritchie dies in Los Angeles.
	Mary Austin and Kathleen Burch found the San Francisco Center for the Book.
1997	Van Velzer and Gotthold relocate Foolscap Press to Santa Cruz.
1998	Lewis Allen dies in Greenbrae.
1999	Carol Twombly, at age 40, retires from Adobe Systems.
	The Zamorano Club auctions off its book collection.
2000	Andrew Hoyem establishes the Grabhorn Institute, San Francisco, to safeguard material inherited from the Grabhorn Press and Mackenzie & Harris.
2001	James Robertson dies in Santa Rosa.
	Under the protection of the Grabhorn Institute, Arion Press and M&H Type relocate to the Presidio of San Francisco.
2003	Sandra Kirshenbaum dies in San Francisco.
2005	Peter Koch and Susan Filter establish the Codex Foundation in Berkeley.
	The Rounce & Coffin Club, Los Angeles, disbands.
2006	Dorothy Allen dies in San Jose.
2007	The Codex Foundation, Berkeley, hosts the first of its biennial international fine press book fairs.

NOTE: For help in compiling and correcting this chronology, I am grateful to Stephen Allen, Charles Bigelow, Elizabeth Fischbach, Madelyn Garrett, Andrew Hoyem, Frederic Marks, Jen Larson at the Center for Book Arts in New York, Carolyn Robertson, the helpful staff at the Bancroft Library, and to all seven of the fine printers whose work is included in this exhibition.

Further Reading

Adams, Ansel. 1978. Conversations with Ansel Adams. Unpublished transcript of 24 interviews conducted in 1972, one in 1974, one in 1975 by Ruth Teiser & Catherine Harroun. Mss BANC 88/82c. Berkeley: Bancroft Library, University of California.

Allen, Lewis M. 1962. "The Evolution of an Edition de Luxe, or: April in Paris." Book Club of California *Quarterly News-Letter* 27.2: 29–34.

———. 1969. *Printing with the Hand Press.* Kentfield, California: Allen Press.

Allen, Lewis, & Dorothy Allen. 1968. Book Printing with the Handpress. Unpublished transcript of an interview conducted in 1968 by Ruth Teiser. Mss BANC 70/22c. Berkeley: Bancroft Library, University of California.

[———]. 1981. *The Allen Press Bibliography: With Artwork [and] Sample Pages from Previous Editions.* Greenbrae, California: Allen Press.

Anderson, Gregg. 1935. *Recollections of the Grabhorn Press.* Meriden, Connecticut: Anderson & Hugo / Los Angeles: Primavera Press. [Reprinted in Anderson 1969.]

———. 1942. *The Work of the Merrymount Press and Its Founder, Daniel Berkeley Updike (1860–1941).* Exhibition catalogue. San Marino: Huntington Library.

———. 1952. "The Books of Edward Bosqui." Pp 167–174 in *Memoirs,* by Edward Bosqui. Oakland: Holmes.

———. 1969. *Two Essays on the Grabhorn Press.* Rochester, N.Y.: Press of the Good Mountain.

[Anderson, Keith, et al.] 1949. *To Remember Gregg Anderson.* [Los Angeles]: "Printed for private circulation."

Anon. [c. 1901?]. *A Few Words about the Stanley-Taylor Company.* [San Francisco: Stanley-Taylor].

Anon., ed. 1980. *California Printing, Part One: 1838–1890.* San Francisco: Book Club of California. [Continued by Johnson & Harlan 1984.]

———, ed. 1980–87. *California Printing: A Select List of Books Which Are Significant or Representative of a California Style of Printing.* 3 vols. San Francisco: Book Club of California.

Archer, H. Richard, & Ward Ritchie. 1968. *Modern Fine Printing: Papers Read at a Clark Library Seminar, March 11, 1967.* Los Angeles: Clark Library.

Bagnall, Jim, et al. 2002. *Remembering James Robertson.* San Francisco: San Francisco Public Library.

Barr, Louise Farrow. 1934. *Presses of Northern California and Their Books, 1900–1933.* Berkeley: Book Arts Club.

Bartlett, Lee, & Allan Campo. 1977. *William Everson: A Descriptive Bibliography, 1934–1976.* Metuchen, N.J.: Scarecrow.

Baughman, Roland O. 1966. "Salute to Edwin and Robert: The Grabhorn Press." *Columbia Library Columns* (New York) 15.2: 23–41. [Reprinted as "The Grabhorns" in *Heritage of the Graphic Arts,* edited by Chandler B. Grannis. New York: Bowker, 1972].

Bender, J. Terry, ed. 1956. *Catalogue of an Exhibition of the Typographic Work of Jane Grabhorn.* Stanford: Stanford University Libraries.

Bentley, Wilder. 1937. *The Printer and the Poet.* Berkeley: Archetype.

———. 1941. "Photography and the Fine Book." *U.S. Camera* (New York) 14: 66–67, 72.

———. [1951?] *Porter Garnett and the Laboratory Press: A Few Philosophical Notes.* Pasadena: Castle Press.

———. 1968. *On a Pedagogical Discovery.* San Francisco: Greenwood Press.

Bigelow, Charles et al., ed. 1989. *Fine Print on Type: The Best of Fine Print Magazine on Type and Typography.* San Francisco: *Fine Print* / Bedford Arts.

Bigus, Richard. 1982. Review of *American Bard* (Lime Kiln Press). *Fine Print* 8.2: 53, 68–69.

Blumenthal, Joseph. 1977. *The Printed Book in America.* Boston: David Godine.

———. 1989. *Bruce Rogers: A Life in Letters, 1870–1957.* Austin, Texas: Taylor.

Bonnani, Vittoria. 2007. "L'arca santa' di Peter Koch al servizio di Fine Art." Pp 541–546 in Pon & Kallendorf.

Bosqui, Edward. 1904. *Memoirs*. San Francisco: privately printed. [Reprinted, with additional material by Henry R. Wagner, Harold C. Holmes, and Gregg Anderson, Oakland: Holmes, 1952.]

Braun, Janice. 2000. Review of *Codex Espangliensis* (Moving Parts Press). *Parenthesis* 4: 33–34.

Bringhurst, Robert. 1993. "Herakleitos in California." *Amphora* (Vancouver) 93: 26–29.

———. 2000. Review of *The Architextures 1–7*, by Nathaniel Tarn (Ninja Press). *Parenthesis* 4 (April 2000): 39–40.

———. 2004. *The Elements of Typographic Style*. 3rd ed. Vancouver: Hartley & Marks.

———. 2008. *Why There Are Pages and Why They Must Turn*. Code(x)+1 Monograph No. 1. Berkeley: Codex Foundation.

———. 2010. "Peter Koch: A Short Introduction." *Amphora* (Vancouver) 155: 3–4.

Bringhurst, Robert, et al. 2003. *Carving the Elements: A Companion to the Fragments of Parmenides*. Berkeley: Editions Koch.

Brown, Scott. 2004. "Peter Koch and the Pre-Socratic Philosophers." *Fine Books & Collections* (Eureka, California) 2.5: 14–15.

Burlingham, Cynthia, & Bruce Whiteman, ed. 2002. *The World from Here: Treasures of the Great Libraries of Los Angeles*. Los Angeles: Grunwald Center/Hammer Museum.

Butler, Francis. 1985. "The Social Economy of the Book." *Fine Print* 11.1: 23–25.

Butor, Michel. 1968. *Inventory*. New York: Simon and Schuster.

Byrne, Chuck. 1998. "Jack W. Stauffacher, Printer, &c." *Emigre* (Sacramento) 45: 16–28.

Campbell, Carolee. 1991. "Thoughts on Ward Ritchie." Pp 8–9 in Glenn et al.

———. 1993. "An Argument for Lying Fallow." *Abracadabra* (Journal of the Alliance for Contemporary Book Arts, Los Angeles) 7: 24.

———. 1994. "Peter Koch, Printer." Book Club of California *Quarterly News-Letter* 60.1: 3–9.

———. 1995. Untitled Statement. *Quarry West* (Santa Cruz) 32: 81.

———. 2000. Untitled Statement, quoted in "A Book Arts Harvest." *Book Club of Washington Journal* (Seattle) 1.2: 3–4.

———. 2005a. "Ninja Press at Twenty." *Matrix* (Andoversford, Gloucestershire) 25: 67–74.

———. 2005b. "The Habit of Risk." College of Creative Studies Commencement Address. *CCS Notes 2005–6* (University of California, Santa Barbara): 10, 23.

Carr, Dan. 2002. "Cutting Parmenides." *Matrix* (Andoversford) 22: 114–129.

Cave, Roderick. 1983. *The Private Press*. 2nd ed. New York: Bowker.

Chappell, Warren, & Robert Bringhurst. 1999. *A Short History of the Printed Word*. 2nd ed. Vancouver: Hartley & Marks.

Clairmont, Corwin, et al. [2005]. *Native Perspectives on the Trail: A Contemporary American Indian Art Portfolio*. Missoula: Missoula Art Museum.

[Cook, Albert S., et al]. 1884. *Catalogue of the Loan Book Exhibition Held at the University of California, Berkeley, May 26th to 31st, 1884*. Exhibition catalogue. Sacramento: James J. Ayers.

Corubolo, Alessandro. 2007. "Da Victor Hammer a Peter Koch: private printers stranieri in Italia." Pp 547–589 in Pon & Kallendorf.

Dahlstrom, Grant Edward. 1982. Impressions from the Castle Press. Unpublished transcript of an interview conducted in 1975 by Richard F. Docter. Mss YRL 300/206. Los Angeles: Oral History Program, ucla.

Daniel, John. 1988. "Turkey Press: No Hardening of the Categories." *Zyzzyva* (San Francisco) 4.1: 132–135.

Davies, David W. 1984. *Bruce McCallister: Los Angeles' First Fine Printer*. Pasadena: Castle Press.

Dean, Malette. 1970. Artist and Printer. Unpublished transcript of interviews conducted in 1969 by Ruth Teiser. Mss BANC 71/109c. Berkeley: Bancroft Library, University of California.

Dickover, Robert. 2007. "James W. Towne, Edward Bosqui, and the Development of Fine Printing in San Francisco." Book Club of California *Quarterly News-Letter* 72.3.

Dimunation, Mark. 2001. "A Printer's Geography: Peter Rutledge Koch, Printer & Typographer." *Imprint* (Journal of the Associates of the Stanford University Libraries) 19.2: 7–25.

Dreyfus, John. 1990. *A Londoner's View of Three Los Angeles Printer Friends and Their Work: Grant Dahlstrom, Saul Marks, and Ward Ritchie*. Los Angeles: Occidental College.

Drucker, Johanna. 1995. *The Century of Artists' Books*. New York. Granary Books.

Elliott, James Welsh. 1985. *Reminiscences of Taylor & Taylor*. San Francisco: Kemble Collection.

———. n.d. Correspondence with Ronald Peters. Peters Collection, Box 32, Ms. Coll. 392, University of Toronto Library.

Elsted, Crispin. 2004. Review of *The Fragments of Parmenides* (Peter Koch). *Parenthesis* 11: 24–26.

Everson, William. [1945?] *The Fine Arts at Waldport*. [Waldport, Oregon: Untide Press].

———. 1966. Brother Antoninus: Poet, Printer, and Religious. Unpublished transcript of interviews conducted in 1965 by Ruth Teiser. Mss BANC 67/92c. Berkeley: Bancroft Library, University of California.

———. 1974. *Archetype West: The Pacific Coast as a Literary Region*. Berkeley: Oyez.

———. 1978. Review of *Ode to Typography*, by Pablo Neruda (Labyrinth Editions). *Fine Print* 4.1: 15.

———. 1980. *Earth Poetry: Selected Essays and Interviews*, edited by Lee Bartlett. Berkeley: Oyez.

———. 1992. *On Printing*, with an introduction by Peter Koch. San Francisco: Book Club of California.

Fahey, Herbert. 1956. *Early Printing in California, from Its Beginning in the Mexican Territory to Statehood, September 9, 1850*. San Francisco: Book Club of California.

FauntLeRoy, Joseph. 1948. *John Henry Nash, Printer*. Oakland: Westgate.

Garnett, Porter. 1994. *Philosophical Writings on the Ideal Book*, edited by Jack Stauffacher. San Francisco: Book Club of California.

Gentry, Linnea. 1975. "On William Everson as Printer." *Fine Print* 1.3: 1–2.

Glenn, Constance W., et al., ed. 1991. *Ward Ritchie: The Laguna Verde Imprenta Years, 1975–1990*. Exhibition catalogue. Long Beach: University Art Museum, California State University.

Gómez-Peña, Guillermo. 2009. "Felicia Rice." Pp 42–44 in *Rydell 2008–2009 Visual Arts Fellows*. Exhibition catalogue. Santa Cruz: Museum of Art & History, McPherson Center.

Goodman, Richard. 2006. "Moving Parts Press." *Fine Books & Collections* (Eureka, California) 19: 26–27.

———. 2008a. "Foolscap Press: Fun with Type." *Fine Books & Collections* (Eureka, California) 33: 30–31.

———. 2008b. "Turkey Press: Slowing Down to Read." *Fine Books & Collections* (Eureka, California) 34: 24–25.

Graalfs, Gregory, & Irene Reti, ed. 2005. The Cowell Press and Its Legacy: Interviews with Jack Stauffacher, George Kane, Aaron Johnson, Peggy Gotthold, Felicia Rice, Tom Killion. Unpublished transcripts of interviews conducted by Graalfs (unnumbered mss, McHenry Library, UC Santa Cruz; UC Berkeley copy: mss BANC 2008/117).

Grabhorn, Edwin E. 1920. *A Chapter from the Lives of Some Noted French Typographers*. San Francisco: Edwin & Robert Grabhorn.

———. 1933. *The Fine Art of Printing: An Address before the Roxburghe Club of San Francisco....* [San Francisco]: E. & R. Grabhorn. [Reprinted in *A Treasury for Typophiles*, edited by Paul Bennett. Cleveland: World, 1963.]

———. 1949. *The Printed Book*. San Francisco: New Harmony Press.

———. 1968. Recollections of the Grabhorn Press. Unpublished transcript of four interviews conducted in 1967 by Ruth Teiser. Mss BANC 69/131c. [Includes a separate interview with Francis Farquhar.] Berkeley: Bancroft Library, University of California.

———. 1969. *Ornamentation in Printing*. San Francisco: Grabhorn-Hoyem.

Grabhorn, Robert. 1968. Fine Printing and the Grabhorn Press. Unpublished transcript of three interviews conducted in 1967 by Ruth Teiser. Mss BANC 69/121c. [Includes a separate interview with Jane Grabhorn.] Berkeley: Bancroft Library, University of California.

———. 1973. *A Printer's Library.* San Francisco: Andrew Hoyem.

Grossman, Carol. 1997. "Arion Press: A Legacy of Literary Artistry." *Biblio* (Eugene, Oregon) 2.9: 30–37.

Grover, Sherwood. 1968. *Life and Hard Times: Or, Sherwood Grover's Twenty-Five Years with Grabhorn Press.* [San Francisco & Los Angeles]: Roxburghe & Zamorano Clubs.

———. 1970. The Grabhorn Press and the Grace Hoper Press. Unpublished transcript of interviews conducted in 1970 by Ruth Teiser, with the participation of Katherine Grover. Mss BANC 74/94c. Berkeley: Bancroft Library, University of California.

———. [1975]. *Malette Dean, Artist and Printer, 1970–1975.* [San Francisco]: Book Club of California.

Grover, Sherwood, & Katherine Grover. 1976. *Presses of the Grabhorn Press.* [San Francisco & Los Angeles]: Roxburghe & Zamorano Clubs.

Harding, George L., ed. 1934. *A Self-Portrait of Captain Agustín V. Zamorano, 1798–1842.* San Francisco: Roxburghe Club.

———. 1973. *Charles A. Murdock, Printer and Citizen of San Francisco: An Appraisal.* Berkeley: Tamalpais Press.

Harlan, Robert D. 1970. *John Henry Nash: The Biography of a Career.* Berkeley: University of California Press. [Continued by Harlan 1982.]

———. 1975. "Oral Histories of San Francisco Printing." *The Library Quarterly* (Chicago) 45.2: 202–205.

———, ed. 1977. *Bibliography of the Grabhorn Press, 1957–66, and Grabhorn-Hoyem, 1966–73.* San Francisco: Grabhorn Press. [Continues Magee & Magee 1957.]

———. 1982. *Chapter Nine: The Vulgate Bible and Other Unfinished Projects of John Henry Nash.* San Francisco: Book Club of California. [Continues Harlan 1970, which consists of 8 chapters.]

———. 1993. *The Two-hundredth Book: A Bibliography of the Books Published by the Book Club of California, 1958–1993.* San Francisco: Book Club of California. [Continues Magee 1958.]

———. 1999. John Henry Nash: Printed Ephemera. Unpublished handlist. Bancroft Library, UC Berkeley.

Harmsen, Tyrus G., & Stephen Tabor. 2005. *The Plantin Press of Saul and Lillian Marks: A Bibliography 1930–1985.* Sebastopol, California: Patrick Reagh.

Harris, Carroll T. 1976. Conversations on Type and Printing. Unpublished transcript of nine interviews conducted in 1967 by Ruth Teiser. Mss BANC 77/54c. Berkeley: Bancroft Library, University of California.

Hart, James D. 1960. *Fine Printing in California.* Berkeley: Tamalpais Press.

———. 1969a. *A Tribute to Edwin Grabhorn and the Grabhorn Press.* San Francisco: Friends of the San Francisco Public Library.

———. 1969b. Fine Printers of the San Francisco Bay Area. Unpublished transcript of an interview conducted in 1969 by Ruth Teiser. Mss BANC 70/188c. Berkeley: Bancroft Library, University of California.

———. 1978. *E&RG: The Grabhorn Brothers.* [Aptos, California]: Sherwood Grover.

———. 1985. *Fine Printing: The San Francisco Tradition.* Washington, D.C.: Library of Congress.

Hart, James D., & Ward Ritchie. 1970. *Influences on California Printing.* Los Angeles: Clark Memorial Library.

Hawk, John, et al. 2001. *Rare Books and Manuscript Collections in the Libraries of the San Francisco Bay Area.* San Francisco: Book Club of California.

Hawks, Nelson Crocker. 1918. *Explanation of the Point System of Printing Type, with Specimens.* Alameda: Island City Press. [Reprinted in facsimile, San Francisco: Black Stone Press, 1983.]

Heller, Elinor R., & David B. Magee. 1940. *Bibliography of the Grabhorn Press, vol. 1: 1915–1940.* San Francisco: [Grabhorn Press]. [Continued by Magee & Magee 1957.]

Hopkins, Rosalind, et al. 1987. *Los Angeles Women Letterpress Printers.* Claremont: Scripps College Press.

Hoyem, Andrew. 1978. A Career in Printing. Untranscribed and unpublished audiotape of a series of interviews conducted by Ruth Teiser. 7 reels. Phonotape 1143a. Berkeley: Bancroft Library, University of California.

[———]. [1985]. *Books, Pamphlets, Portfolios Designed, Printed, Published by Andrew Hoyem during 25 Years....* [Columbus, Ohio]: Ohio State University Libraries.

[———]. [1995]. *Catalogue 1995–1975: Retrospective Checklist of Publications [of] the Arion Press.* San Francisco: Arion Press.

———. 2010. "Traditional Texts in New Formats." *Parenthesis* 19: 21–25.

Humphreys, Glenn E. 1987. "Printing, Publishing, and Ancillary Trades: A Checklist of Manuscript and Archival Holdings in the Edward C. Kemble Collections on Western Printing & Publishing." *California History* 66.1: 55–67.

Hunt, Haywood. 1967. Recollections of San Francisco Printers. Unpublished transcript of an interview conducted in 1966 by Ruth Teiser. Mss BANC 68/95c. Berkeley: Bancroft Library, University of California.

Hurewitz, Daniel. 2007. *Bohemian Los Angeles and the Making of Modern Politics.* Berkeley: University of California Press.

Jackson, Robert H., & Carol Z. Rothkopf, ed. 2006. *Book Talk: Essays on Books, Booksellers, Collecting, and Special Collections.* New Castle, Delaware: Oak Knoll.

Jaeger, Roland. 2000. *New Weimar on the Pacific: The Pazifische Presse and German Exile Publishing in Los Angeles, 1942–1948.* Los Angeles: Victoria Dailey.

Johnck, John J. 1932. *The Principles Underlying Typography.* Seattle: Dogwood Press.

Johnson, Bruce L. 2008. *James Weld Towne: Pioneer San Francisco Printer, Publisher, & Paper Merchant.* San Francisco: Book Club of California.

Johnson, Bruce L., & Robert D. Harlan, ed. 1984. *California Printing, Part Two: 1890–1925.* San Francisco: Book Club of California. [Continues Anon. 1980; continued by Kirshenbaum & Karmiole 1987.]

Johnson, Robert Flynn, & Donna Stein. 2001. *Artists' Books in the Modern Era, 1870–2000: The Reva and David Logan Collection of Illustrated Books.* San Francisco: Fine Arts Museums of San Francisco.

[Johnston, Alastair]. 1976. *A Bibliography of the Auerhahn Press and Its Successor Dave Haselwood Books.* Berkeley: Poltroon Press.

———. 1979. "Jack Werner Stauffacher, Typographer." *Fine Print* 5.1: 1–6.

———. 1995. "The Robert Grabhorn Collection on the History of Printing and the Development of the Book at SFPL." *Bookways* (Austin, Texas) 15/16: 52–59.

Juarez, Miguel. 2006. "The Culture of the Book: Ninja Press at Twenty, 1984–2004." *Art Documentation* (Bulletin of the Art Libraries Society of North America) 25.2: 30–33.

Jury, David, ed. 2008. *Book Art Object.* Berkeley: Codex Foundation.

Kennedy, Lawton. 1967. A Life in Printing. Unpublished transcript of five interviews conducted in 1966 by Ruth Teiser. Mss BANC 69/78c. Berkeley: Bancroft Library, University of California.

Kirshenbaum, Sandra, ed. 1979. *Five Fine Printers: Jack Stauffacher, Adrian Wilson, Richard Bigus, Andrew Hoyem, William Everson.* Exhibition catalogue. Davis: University of California, Davis.

———. 1985. "A Decennary Letter from the Publisher." *Fine Print* 11.1: 3–10.

———. 2001. A Life with Books and with Fine Print: A Review for the Arts of the Book. Unpublished transcript of four interviews conducted in 1999 by Robert D. Harlan. Mss BANC 2002/86c. Berkeley: Bancroft Library, University of California.

Kirshenbaum, Sandra, & Kenneth Karmiole, ed. 1987. *California Printing, Part Three: 1925–1975.* San Francisco: Book Club of California. [Continues Johnson & Harlan 1984.]

Knuttel, Gerard. 1951. *The Letter as a Work of Art.* Amsterdam: Tetterode.

Koch, Peter Rutledge. 1989. Review of *Her Six Difficulties and His Small Mistakes* (Labyrinth Editions). *Fine Print* 15.2: 62.

———. 2004. "Philosophy and Printing in the Real West, or: Herakleitos in Montana & Diogenes on Telegraph Avenue." Pp 19–33 in Bringhurst et al., *Carving the Elements.*

———. 2006a. "The Pre-Socratic Project and Remarks on the Philosophical Side of Fine Printing." Pp 39–55 in Jackson & Rothkopf.

———. 2006b. "On Ephemeral Printing." Pp [5–7] in *The Koch Ephemera: A Selection from the Archive.* Chapbook accompanying a portfolio of printed ephemera. Berkeley: [Peter Koch].

———. 2007. "Printing in the Shadow of Aldus: The Book as a Work of Art in the Twenty-First Century." Pp 535–540 in Pon & Kallendorf.

———. 2008. *Art: Definition Five (and Other Writings).* Code(x)+1 Monograph No. 2. Berkeley: Codex Foundation.

———. 2010a. "Three Philosophical Printers: William Everson, Jack Stauffacher, and Adrian Wilson." *Parenthesis* 19: 12–17.

———. 2010b. "Fine Printing in the San Francisco Bay Area." Interview. *Parenthesis* 19: 34–36.

Koch, Peter Rutledge, et al. 1995a. *Peter Koch, Printer: Surrealist Cowboys, Maverick Poets, and Presocratic Philosophers.* Exhibition catalogue. New York & San Francisco: New York Public Library & San Francisco Public Library.

———. 1995b. *Peter Koch, Printer: Recent Work.* Exhibition catalogue. Cambridge, Mass.: Houghton Library, Harvard University.

———. 2004. *Nature Morte.* Exhibition catalogue. Helena: Holter Museum.

Koch, Peter, & Susan Filter. 2008. "Printing in the Shadow of Aldus." *Parenthesis* 15: 12–17. [Not the same as Koch 2007, despite the identical title.]

Krayna, Philip. 1999. "History, Unfolded." *Print* (New York) 53.1: 90–93.

Lange, Gerald. 2001. *Printing Digital Type on the Hand-Operated Flatbed Cylinder Press.* 2nd ed. Marina del Rey: Bieler Press.

———. 2010. Review of *The Persephones,* by Nathaniel Tarn (Ninja Press). *Parenthesis* 19: 57–59.

Lauf, Cornelia and Clive Phillpot, eds. 1998. *Artist / Author: Contemporary Artists' Books.* New York. American Federation of Arts.

Lerner, Abe. 1979. *Assault on the Book: A Critique of Fine Printing at Private Presses in the United States Today.* [North Hills, Pennsylvania]: Bird & Bull Press.

Lewis, Oscar. 1930. "The California School of Printing." *The Colophon* (New York) 1.3: [8 pp, unnumbered].

———. 1946. *Fine Printing in the Far West.* Orinda, California: Platen Press. [Originally published in 1926.]

———. 1965. Literary San Francisco. Unpublished transcript of four interviews conducted in 1965 by Ruth Teiser & Catherine Harroun. Mss BANC C-D 4099. Berkeley: Bancroft Library, University of California.

———. 1987. *The First Seventy-Five Years: The Story of the Book Club of California.* San Francisco: Book Club of California.

Livingston, Mark. 1984. "The Yolla Bolly Press." *Fine Print* 10.2: 56–60.

McGurk, Ruth, et al. 1995. *Dressing the Text: The Fine Press Artists' Book.* Exhibition catalogue. Santa Cruz: Printers' Chappel of Santa Cruz.

McVarish, Emily. 1998. Review of *Codex Espangliensis* (Moving Parts Press). *Journal of Artists' Books* (Chicago) 10: 22–24.

Magee, David B. 1958. *The Hundredth Book: A Bibliography of the Publications of the Book Club of California and a History of the Club.* San Francisco: Book Club of California. [Continued by Harlan 1993.]

———. 1960. *Catalogue of Some Five Hundred Examples of the Printing of Edwin and Robert Grabhorn, 1917–1960: The Two Gentlemen from Indiana Now Resident in California.* San Francisco: [Grabhorn Press].

———. 1961. *Fine Printing and Bookbinding from San Francisco.* Exhibition catalogue. San Francisco: Grabhorn Press.

Magee, Dorothy, & David Magee. 1957. *Bibliography of the Grabhorn Press, vol. 2: 1940–56.* San Francisco: Grabhorn Press.

[Continues Heller & Magee 1940; continued by Harlan 1977.]

Marks, Lillian. 1980. *Saul Marks and the Plantin Press: The Life and Work of a Singular Man.* Los Angeles: Plantin Press.

———. 1989. *On Printing in the Tradition.* Sacramento: California State Library Foundation.

Maryatt, Kitty. 2010. "In Full Force: The Scripps College Press." *Parenthesis* 19: 33–34.

Mostardi, David. 2001. *A Checklist of the Publications of Paul Elder.* Olalla, Washington: Arts & Crafts Press.

Murdock, Charles A. 1910. "An Appreciation of the Work of John Henry Nash." *American Bulletin* (Journal of the American Type Founders Co.) 1.

Muto, Albert. 1992. *The University of California Press: The Early Years, 1893–1953.* Berkeley: University of California Press.

Nelson, Victoria. 1988. "Stones on the Riverbed: Jack Stauffacher's Typographic Art." *Fine Print* 14.2: 92–93.

Nixon, Bruce. 2005. *Manuel Neri: Artists' Books/The Collaborative Process.* San Francisco: Fine Arts Museums / Manchester, Vermont: Hudson Hills.

O'Day, Nell. 1937. *A Catalogue of Books Printed by John Henry Nash.* San Francisco: [John Henry Nash].

Peyré, Yves. 2001. *Peinture et poésie: le dialogue par le livre, 1874–2000.* Paris: Gallimard.

Pon, Lisa, & Craig Kallendorf, ed. 2007. *The Books of Venice / Il Libro Veneziano.* Miscellanea Marciana 20. Venice: Biblioteca nazionale Marciana.

Powell, Lawrence Clark. 1997. *The Work of Ward Ritchie, Designer, Printer, Poet: His Alter Ego and His Muses.* Tucson: Truepenny.

Prestianni, John. 1993. "A Scribe's Treasure: Calligraphy in the San Francisco Public Library." *Calligraphy Review* (Norman, Okla.) 10.4: 34–45.

Randle, John. 2004. Review of *XXIV Short Love Poems,* by Bruce Whiteman (Ninja Press). *Matrix* (Andoversford) 24: 156.

Reese, Harry. 1981. "Poetics and Technology: Towards a Typography of the 1980s." *Scree* (Fallon, Nevada) 17/18: 97–103.

———. 1987. *The Sandragraph: Between Printing and Painting.* Los Angeles: Arundel Press.

———. 1994. "The Book as Site, Public Art, and Media Ecology." *Abracadabra* (Journal of the Alliance for Contemporary Book Arts, Los Angeles) 8: 26–30.

———. 1998. "The Tactility of Artists' Books." Pp 25–32 in *Making Artist Books Today,* edited by Wulf D. von Lucius & Gunnar A. Kaldewey. Stuttgart: Lucius & Lucius.

Rice, Felicia, ed. 1995. *The Poet as Printer: William Everson and the Fine Press Artist's Book.* Special issue. *Quarry West* (Santa Cruz) 32.

———. 2001. "Codex Espangliensis." *Journal of Artists' Books* (Chicago) 15: 20–21.

Rice, Felicia, & Betsy Miller. 1994. "Conversations: Felicia Rice, Santa Cruz, California." *Bookways* (Austin, Texas) 12: 32–33, 41–44.

Riese, Renée, & Judd Hubert. 2000. "L'art du livre: l'apport californien." *Revue No 1* (Saint-Yrieix-la-Perche, Limousin: Centre des Livres d'Artistes): 28–30. [On Ninja Press.]

Ritchie, Ward. 1969. Printing and Publishing in Southern California. Unpublished transcript of a series of interviews conducted in 1964–6 by Elizabeth Dixon. Mss YRL 300/67. Los Angeles: Oral History Program, UCLA.

———. 1980. *The Poet and the Printers.* [Laguna Beach]: Laguna Verde.

———. 1984. *A Concise Account of Ward Ritchie: His Printing and His Books,* edited by David W. Davies. Los Angeles: Dawson's Book Shop.

———. 1987a. *Fine Printing: The Los Angeles Tradition.* Washington, D.C.: Library of Congress.

———. 1987b. *Art Deco: The Books of François-Louis Schmied, Artist/Engraver/Printer.* San Francisco: Book Club of California.

———. 1988. *Fine Printers: The New Generation in Southern California.* Sacramento: California State Library Foundation.

———. 1989. *Of Bookmen and Printers: A Gathering of Memories.* Los Angeles: Dawsons.

———. 1996. *A Southland Bohemia: The Arroyo Seco Colony as the Century Begins.* Pasadena: Weather Bird Press.

Rogers, Bruce. 1912. "Progress of Modern Printing in the United States." *The Times* (London) September 10, 1912: 18. [Reprinted in *Pi: A Hodge-Podge of the Letters, Papers and Addresses Written During the Last Sixty Years*. Cleveland & New York: World, 1953.]

Rosenthal, Bernard. 1982. *Wilder Bentley the Elder at the Archetype Press*. San Francisco: Arion Press.

Ryan, Michael T. 1992. *The Coming of the Book Arts to the Farm*. [San Francisco: Roxburghe Club; Los Angeles: Zamorano Club; Palo Alto: Stanford University Libraries].

Schoonover, David. 2010. Review of *Herakles and the Eurystheusian Twelve-Step Program* (Foolscap Press). *Parenthesis* 19: 61–62.

Shasky, Florian J., & Joanne Sonnichsen et al. 1994. *Hand Bookbinding in California: A Keepsake in Twelve Parts*. San Francisco: Book Club of California.

Starr, Kevin. 1990. *Material Dreams: Southern California through the 1920s*. New York: Oxford University Press.

Stauffacher, Jack W. 1969. A Printed Word Has Its Own Measure. Unpublished transcript of an interview conducted in 1968 by Ruth Teiser. Mss BANC 70/139c. Berkeley: Bancroft Library, University of California.

———. 1978. *A Search for the Typographic Form of Plato's Phaedrus*. San Francisco: Greenwood Press.

———. 1996. The Word, Bearer of Our Confessions: The Greenwood Press 1968–1996. Unpublished transcript of four interviews conducted in 1996 by Robert Harlan. Mss BANC 98/92c. Berkeley: Bancroft Library, University of California.

———. 1999. *A Typographic Journey: The History of the Greenwood Press and Bibliography, 1934–2000*. San Francisco: Book Club of California.

Stauffacher, Jack W., & Michael Taylor. 1992. *The Continuity of Horace*. San Francisco: Greenwood Press.

[Taylor, Henry Huntly, & Edward DeWitt Taylor]. 1917. "A Statement of the Policy of This House." *T & T Imprint* (San Francisco) 16. [Reprinted as *A Reprint of the Taylor and Taylor Imprint for the Winter MCMXVI–VII*. San Rafael: Mt Tam Press / Petaluma: Anchor & Acorn Press, 1988.]

[———]. 1939. *Type, Borders and Miscellany of Taylor & Taylor: With Historical Brevities on Their Derivation and Use*. Specimen book. San Francisco: Taylor & Taylor.

Taylor, W. Thomas. 1979. Review of *Five Fine Printers* (exhibition and catalogue). *Fine Print* 5.3: 84–85.

Teiser, Ruth. 1988. *Lawton Kennedy, Printer, 1900–1980*. San Francisco: Book Club of California.

Teiser, Ruth, & Catherine Harroun, ed. 1970. *Printing as a Performing Art*. San Francisco: Book Club of California.

Towne, James Weld. 1981. *A Promise Unfulfilled: Being a Letter from James W. Towne, San Francisco, 1866*. San Francisco: Friends of the Kemble Collection.

Updike, Daniel Berkeley. 1924. *In the Day's Work*. Cambridge, Mass: Harvard University Press.

———. 1937. *Printing Types: Their History, Forms, and Use*. 2nd ed. 2 vols. Cambridge, Mass: Harvard University Press.

Van Velzer, Lawrence G. 2002. "The Tower of the Winds: A Scroll Book." *Tabellae Ansatae* (Greensboro, NC) 2.3: 8–9.

Wells, James M. 1966. "Book Typography in the United States of America." Pp 325–370 in *Book Typography 1815–1965: In Europe and the United States of America*, edited by Kenneth Day. London: Ernest Benn.

Wentz, Roby. 1981. *The Grabhorn Press: A Biography*. San Francisco: Book Club of California.

Whiteman, Bruce. 2007. "Moving Parts Press." *Parenthesis* 13: 35–37.

Williams, Griff. 2000. *Hard Words: Peter Rutledge Koch*. Exhibition catalogue. San Francisco: Gallery 16 / Missoula: University of Montana Art Galleries.

Wilson, Adrian. 1957. *Printing for Theater*. San Francisco: Adrian Wilson.

———. 1966. Printing and Book Designing. Unpublished transcript of an interview conducted in 1965 by Ruth Teiser. Mss BANC C-D 4107. Berkeley: Bancroft Library, University of California.

———. 1967. *The Design of Books*. New York: Reinhold.

———. 1983. *The Work and Play of Adrian Wilson: A Bibliography with Commentary*, edited by Joyce Lancaster Wilson. Austin, Texas: W. Thomas Taylor.

———. 1990. *Two against the Tide: A Conscientious Objector in World War II: Selected Letters 1941–1948*, edited by Joyce Lancaster Wilson. Austin, Texas: W. Thomas Taylor.

Wilson, Murray D. 1976. *Modern Fine Printers of the Small Press: Clifford Burke, Don Gray, Andrew Hoyem, Noel Young.* Minneapolis: University of Minnesota.

Winter, Don. 1985. Los Angeles Type Founders, Inc. Unpublished transcript of an interview conducted in 1979 by Nancy Sue Skipper. Mss YRL 300/257. Los Angeles: Oral History Program, ucla.

Woodall, Steve. 1998. *Out West: The Artist's Book in California, Part 1: Northern California.* Exhibition catalogue. New York: Center for Book Arts. [The second part of the exhibition, devoted to Southern California, was mounted in 2001, but Part 2 of the catalogue was never published.]

Wulling, Emerson G. 1983. *A Comp's-Eye View of Wilder Bentley and the Archetype Press.* La Crosse, Wisconsin: Sumac Press.

Young, Gary. 2010. "The Book Club of California at 100." *Parenthesis* 19: 28–29.

Zeitlin, Jacob. 1956. "Small Renaissance, Southern California Style." *Papers of the Bibliographical Society of America* 50: 17–27.

Design and typography by Peter Rutledge Koch. Jonathan Gerken, assistant designer.

This book is typeset in Espinosa Nova, by Cristóbal Henestrosa, first issued in 2010 by Estudio-CH, Mexico City, DF. The design is based on types originally cut by Antonio de Espinosa and first used in Alonso de la Vera Cruz's *Recognitio Svmmularum* (1554). These were the first roman types cut and printed in the New World.